Restructuring Schools

HOW TO ORDER THIS BOOK

BY PHONE: 800-233-9936 or 717-291-5609, 8AM–5PM Eastern Time

BY FAX: 717-295-4538

BY MAIL: Order Department
Technomic Publishing Company, Inc.
851 New Holland Avenue, Box 3535
Lancaster, PA 17604, U.S.A.

BY CREDIT CARD: American Express, VISA, MasterCard

Restructuring Schools

THEORY AND PRACTICE

Charles A. Reavis
Texas Tech University

Harry Griffith
Goose Creek Independent School District

TECHNOMIC
PUBLISHING CO., INC.

LANCASTER · BASEL

Restructuring Schools

ₐ TECHNOMIC® publication

Published in the Western Hemisphere by
Technomic Publishing Company, Inc.
851 New Holland Avenue
Box 3535
Lancaster, Pennsylvania 17604 U.S.A.

Distributed in the Rest of the World by
Technomic Publishing AG

Printed in the United States of America
10 9 .8 7 6 5 4 3 2

Main entry under title:
  Restructuring Schools: Theory and Practice

A Technomic Publishing Company book
Bibliography: p.
Includes index p. 219

Library of Congress Card No. 91-66130
ISBN No. 87762-849-1

CONTENTS

[1] Introduction to Restructuring

The restructuring groundswell has finally become a tidal wave. The current restructuring movement may be traced to the shift by large urban school districts toward decentralization in the 1960s. Another hallmark was Rist's book published in 1972, *Restructuring American Education*, which was largely ignored at the time. Calls for school reform have continued, however, so that now restructuring is promoted by such diverse advocates as David Kearns of the Xerox Corporation, Albert Shanker of the American Federation of Teachers, and President Bush, along with assorted governors.

While the renewed interest in restructuring is most welcome, there are also many caveats to observe. In the past, for example, some educators have claimed to be implementing an innovation while actually engaging in numerous practices that only marginally reflected the power of the original concept. Already there are indications that this is happening with respect to restructuring. The term is being applied equally to the radical citizen-controlled school committees of the Chicago schools and to the relatively mild interventions in which one school is permitted to pilot site-based decision making in a few non-controversial decision areas. Radical interventions or mild pilots have the potential of neutralizing the potency of restructuring. If this were to occur, the schools would miss what might prove to be their last opportunity to self-correct. The demands for vastly improved schools are too compelling to fade away. The current pressing issue is to prepare school administrators sufficiently to enable them to lead the new wave of reform. To lead that reform, the school administrator must have a firm grasp of the difference between restructuring, decentralizing, and site-based management.

Restructuring, Decentralizing, Site-Based Management

Restructuring

Restructuring is in danger of losing its intended meaning. Accord-

1

ing to Michael Kirst, "Restructuring is a word that means everything and nothing simultaneously. . . . It is in the eye of the beholder" [1]. Similarly, Goodlad has said, "We are rapidly moving toward the use of the word 'restructuring' whenever we talk about school reform at all. . . . This is becoming another catchword when the truth of the matter is that hardly any schools are restructured" [1].

What, then, is restructuring? It means a complete change in the culture, organizational assumptions, leadership, curriculum, instructional approach, and accountability of the school. Ideas of how things get done, work norms, decision making, authority, motivation, and professional expertise all must be radically revised, as will be shown in this and subsequent chapters. To illustrate, restructuring means decision making by the person closest to the issue to be resolved. It means wide participation in a number of areas that have traditionally been reserved as the prerogative of building or central office administrators. For example, in Chaparrel Elementary School, in Albuquerque, N.M., the principal is not involved in interviewing and hiring teachers; the teachers at the school are solely responsible for this.

Further, restructuring requires access to information and resources. It requires the learning of new roles by administrators, teachers, students, parents, and members of the community at large. Perhaps most of all, it requires the adoption of a market orientation in which the customers are the parents and the students. In short, restructuring means exactly what the name implies—a complete change in the structure of the organization and the underlying beliefs that have given rise to that organization. Nationwide, a consensus is beginning to emerge on the seven elements of restructuring.

(1) Site-based decision making in the critical areas of budget, staff development, curriculum and instruction, and personnel

(2) A shift to a market-driven orientation, usually on the basis of parental choice of school

(3) An increase in and shift in the focus of technology use, from simple drill to an integrated instructional package [2]

(4) A shift in instructional emphasis to conform more closely to new understandings of human cognition

(5) A shift in curriculum from an emphasis on coverage of a wide range of topics to an emphasis on understanding and assisting students in constructing their own meaning

(6) A shift to hierarchies within teaching, reflecting differing levels of responsibilities with various sizes of student groups

(7) A change in accountability toward more performance-oriented/ real-life assessments of students

Far from being an insignificant movement in education, a fad, evidence is mounting that restructuring represents a major policy shift. A recent survey of the Council of Chief State School Officers lists thirty states that have by legislation implemented one or more aspects of restructuring [3].

Decentralization and Site-Based Management

In contrast to the complete change in roles, organizational structure, and culture that is required for successful restructuring, decentralization and site-based management merely involve a change in the source of decisions. Decentralizing is usually found in large districts. In order to make them more manageable, sub-districts are organized within the larger district. There is little or no challenge to prevailing organizational assumptions or bureaucratic structures, and little or no increase in opportunities for decision making by teachers, students, and parents. Site-based management takes decentralization one step further by, in effect, "decentralizing" decision making to each building. In most such arrangements, provision will be made for some teacher participation in decisions, usually in the area of curriculum. However, since no change is required in the behaviors of central office personnel, the opportunity for significant organizational change is not great.

It has been said that the enemy of the best is the "good enough." The danger of timid experiments in site-based management is that they will prove "good enough" to relax the pressure for substantial organizational change. It is the organizational constraints and assumptions, not the professionals in the organization, that so limit school effectiveness.

Organizational Constraints on School Effectiveness

Problems with Bureaucracies—Human

Max Weber [4] described the characteristics of the ideal bureaucratic organization. He believed that "the decisive reason for the advance of bureaucratic organization has always been its purely technical superiority over other forms of organization." Weber's ideal bureaucracy consisted of a division of labor; hierarchical levels of authority; action based on written policies, rules and regulations; an impersonal environment; and career orientation. The strength of the bureaucratic organization is the orderliness and efficiency that it brings to administration. Use of bureaucratic principles of organization has enabled schools to educate large numbers of children in the past.

To work most efficiently, however, the schools must make assumptions about the students to be educated. The students must be sufficiently uniform to be "batch processed," or they must be pliable enough so they can be shaped for batch processing. In a similar vein, teachers must either be uniform or must be pliable enough that they can be batch processed. As long as these assumptions hold, the bureaucratic organization can be both efficient and effective. However, students are becoming increasingly diverse through immigration, changing social mores, and access to external technological resources such as computers and television. Similarly, teachers are no longer the compliant, lower-middle-class females that for decades filled the ranks of teaching.

Problems with Bureaucracies—Organizational

Turning from human to organizational considerations, some have charged that the bureaucratic principles have been applied too generally in schools. Weick [5], for example, has suggested that in matters of curriculum and instruction, schools should be "loosely coupled," avoiding the tightly coupled structure that would be required by a strict bureaucratic organization. Loose coupling in matters of curriculum, for example, would permit teachers to adjust the curriculum, within limits, to the needs, interests, and readiness levels of the students.

In a different analysis, McNeil [6] sees schools operating under the factory model, carefully producing compliant workers for the factories of the 19th century. Excessive emphasis on control, she writes, has served to induce teachers to engage in defensive teaching (teaching from lists, smoothing over potentially controversial material, omitting material that was difficult) in a non-verbalized compact with students ("I won't make this difficult if you will comply with my expectations."). While such an outcome is not the intent of bureaucratic organizations, an emphasis on control is a natural consequence of bureaucratic organizational principles, which gravitate toward orderliness and routine. The irony of an emphasis on control, McNeil charges, is that it defeats the very objective that the bureaucracy was created to promote originally—the creation of an educated individual.

A third organizational constraint is that bureaucracies, left to themselves, tend to become increasingly self-serving; that is, they tend to try to increase efficiency and lose sight of the objectives they are pursuing. Other charges regarding the limitations of bureaucratic organizations are that the emphasis on rules and precedents limits teacher creativity and entrepreneurship. Teacher and subject isolation that is a result of specialization further limits the education of students, according to Sizer [7] because these tend to contribute to a fragmented curriculum that leaves students with bits and pieces of information. Sizer noted that when a new specialty develops in law, for example, the faculty doesn't hire a specialist – someone simply develops that area. In current schools, bureaucracies would create a new specialty and add a certification.

The reason for the limitations of the typical school organization, according to Kanter [8], is that they are excessively segmented. Segmentation typically permits only modest departures from conventional practice. This appears to occur because members of segmented organizations do not have an overall picture to permit a fundamental change in the organization to accommodate the suggested innovation. Thus the innovation is placed in a hostile or unaccommodating environment with little chance of survival. In education we have witnessed the "bandwagon" effect – an innovation is introduced with high hopes, only to fade in the enthusiasm for the next innovation. The succession of failed innovations was predictable, according to Kanter, due to excessive organizational segmentation.

Thus segmentation, which follows from bureaucratic specialization, almost insures the failure of innovation. The 1990 National Assessment of Educational Progress revealed no gains in achievement in either reading or writing since the first test in 1974. Commenting on the results, former Secretary of Education Cavazos said the test results clearly call for organizational change at an "elemental, fundamental level." In other words, in spite of fifteen years marked by numerous innovative programs in both reading and writing, the message has to be clear that yet more innovative programs are not the answer. There must be something more fundamentally flawed with the educational process. Insights by Kanter, McNeil, and others are beginning to define that "something" as the bureaucratic process. Important to note here is that the bureaucratic organization was effective in achieving objectives in the early part of this century – the teaching of basic skills to the upper 30 to 40 percent of the children. However, to prepare children to work in an information society, different objectives are required and different structures are necessary to insure the attainment of those objectives.

Rationale for Restructuring

A number of rationales have been developed in support of restructuring. David Kearns [9], CEO of Xerox Corporation, has urged restructuring as a means of heightening the market sensitivity of educators. In his view, there is currently no penalty for poor performance by schools. Poor schools continue to be funded on the same basis as other schools in the district, and get their same allotment of students. Therefore, there is little incentive for low-achieving schools to improve services. Further, they can blame their lack of success on external rules, requirements, and mandates. If they were given more autonomy with commensurate responsibility, he reasons, they would have to improve or else go out of business as parents chose other, more effective schools for their children. Thus, market forces would exercise leverage on schools as they currently do in the business world.

Albert Shanker [10] and The Task Force on the Teaching Profession of the Carnegie Forum on Education and the Economy [11] support restructuring, not in order to introduce market forces into education, but rather to empower educators as the knowledgeable professionals in education. Freeing educators from external constraints and organizational disincentives, they argue, would motivate them to the highest levels of commitment and creativity to design schools for the 21st century.

In writing of organizations of the 21st century, Drucker [12] discusses the organizational structure that will be found in an information-based age. The structure will be much flatter, he argues, because most middle managers currently function as "information relays" – human boosters for the faint signals that characterize the bureaucratic organization. As information becomes available to those closest to the level at which the decision must be made, and as they are empowered to make decisions, there will be less need for intermediaries.

Some would hold that we will not have to wait for the 21st century for such organizations to appear. O'Toole [13] has written about vanguard organizations that utilize human resources principles to extend dignity and participation in organizational decisions to even the lowliest employee. His vanguard companies have an enviable record of adjusting to economic fluctuations, competition, shifts in customer preferences, and so forth. An important point here is that O'Toole's vanguard companies utilize teams, not committees, of employees as a central mechanism of restructuring.

Teamwork—Central to Restructuring

A popular and particularly American tradition is the achievement of excellence by an individual through a high level of commitment, vision, and drive. Recently in education we have witnessed the celebration of the achievements of Jaime Escalante, Marva Collins, and George McKenna. However, the organization of the future will achieve its effects by the focused, collective efforts of empowered professional teams, according to Reich, writing in the *Harvard Business Review*. He elaborates,

> Competitive advantage today comes from continuous, incremental innovation and refinement of a variety of ideas that spread throughout the organization. The entrepreneurial organization is both experience-based and decentralized, so that every advance builds on every previous advance, and everyone in the company has the opportunity and capacity to participate.

He continues by stating that companies of the future must "Involve everyone in the organization in a systemwide search for ways to improve, adjust, adapt, and upgrade" [14].

Characteristics of a Restructuring System

Characteristics from the Rationale

From the rationale above, certain characteristics of the restructured system emerge.

- It will be a flatter organization with fewer levels of management between the superintendent and the teachers.
- Most management levels will function as coordinators to facilitate the work of groups, as opposed to acting as compliance monitors and evaluators.
- Decisions will be made by groups and will be made at the lowest possible level in the organization.
- Because many decisions will be made at the school level, much more diversity will be observed from school to school within the same district.

- Coupled with a greater latitude in the instructional process by which outcomes are to be achieved, an accountability for student achievement must be established that uses a broader index than mere standardized achievement test scores. Other sources of information might be drop-out and attendance rates, student projects, and standardized tests of creativity and self-esteem.
- Teachers must assume (must be trusted to assume) substantially more responsibility for total school organizational reform (not merely curriculum reform).
- Collaborative relationships between teachers and building administrators must supersede hierarchical ones.
- Contributions to student learning must become the primary basis upon which decisions are made rather than tradition or bureaucratic convenience.
- Strenuous efforts must constantly be exerted to examine all assumptions about the organization itself. Typically this will mean that anything that promotes segmentation and isolation will be rigorously scrutinized. If not absolutely necessary, it will be eliminated.

Characteristics from the Literature

In addition to the factors above that flow from the rationale for restructuring, a number of other characteristics have emerged in the literature as requisite for restructuring.

A clear statement of outcome expectations must be articulated by the central office. These will set the broad parameters that will guide the entrepreneurial activities at the individual schools. These should be broad and focus on a wide range of outcomes to include problem solving, higher-level thinking skills, working cooperatively in teams, cross-cultural understanding, creativity, self-discipline, academic skills, communication, and so forth.

Leaders must become skillful in and committed to developing the full potential in their subordinates. Strong and continuing in-service education must be provided to keep educators informed of materials, instructional options, and technological advances that they may potentially utilize. It would be useless to provide teachers more opportunities for decision making if the knowledge of options were narrowly constricted.

A high moral commitment must be developed to provide the best possible education to all students. The conviction that success is limited to the fortunate few dies hard because it tends to be embedded in organizational assumptions and practices. A deep conviction that all students can learn must be fostered.

A reward system must be developed that recognizes the contributions of teachers on a broad index, such as that proposed by Shulman [15]. Writing about his work for the Teacher Assessment Project, he suggests a written test on content and pedagogy; assessment center exercises requiring the teacher to demonstrate skill in specified teaching functions (planning, for example) in a controlled setting; field documentation of specified teaching functions by a mentor and including portfolios of teacher and student work; and classroom observations to verify the quality of decision making, particularly regarding the decision of when to use the functions. Such a reward system is necessary because not all teachers are either willing or able to make an investment commitment to school objectives [16]. All organizational administrators need to recognize that leadership is widespread in the organization [17].

Local school culture must be analyzed in order to surface subtle organizational blocks to genuine improvement. Informal norms and traditions of non-involvement can prevent the participation vital to restructuring. There must be a genuine willingness to confront sacred cows and to test these against a standard of research support, commitment, and service to children.

Schools must establish moral authority (not legal or quasi-legal authority) as their basis for power. This is necessary because a moral basis usually carries a great deal of motivational power. This moral basis implies that parents who entrust their children to us do so with the expectation that we will exercise the highest levels of professional judgement. It is not too much to say that the whole future of the student body rests on our deep commitment to providing the very best services possible for each child. Failure to establish a moral basis may result in a situation where teachers and others brought into the decision-making process make self-serving decisions.

There must be a shift from an exclusive focus on short-term goals that can be measured by machine-scored standardized tests to long-term goals similar to those described by Honig, the superintendent of the California public schools. The new tests are labeled "authentic assessments" because they ask students to show that they can write, think, solve problems, and complete experiments under conditions that mirror the real world. Honig continues, ". . . Teaching to these tests is what we want, because the tests are 100% connected with real-world, on-the-job performance. We're finished with tests that measure only isolated, low-level 'basic' skills" [18]. This shift in measurement of student achievement is required because the school organization that is being created is designed to produce students with knowledge and skills for success in the 21st century. These are quite different from those tested by current standardized tests, and will be discussed further in Chapter 4.

Cautions Regarding Restructuring

Most school leaders have no experience in creating or leading a market-driven organization. While some will doubtless be able to start and feel their way along, many others will need initial training with support during implementation, perhaps by networking with other like-minded school leaders.

Teachers may be uncomfortable functioning as decision makers with the accompanying responsibility to produce results that this entails. They may be expected initially to engage in redelegation back to the building administrator and central office. This may be used by some to prove that teachers don't really wish to have a role in decision making. However, teachers have been subject to the same bureaucratic traditions as administrators, and can be expected to experience similar feelings of discomfort in some phases of the restructuring process.

Boards and the general public may not accept the broader index of student outcomes as readily as they currently accept the convenience of a few numerical averages provided by standardized test scores. However, building an organization for the 21st century requires measurement of skills, behaviors, and attitudes that will help students to be successful in the 21st century. Part of the job of all school leaders is to assist parents, board members and the community in understanding and accepting the broader measures of school success. These broader goals (such as problem-solving skills) may be easy to identify, but difficult to hold schools and teachers accountable for.

Many traditions will prove tenacious, and may resurface in a new guise. Thus school administrators must be highly vigilant in anticipating and recognizing bureaucratic tendencies, exposing them, and eliminating them. A regression to bureaucratic controls is a constant danger. Particularly in the early stages of restructuring, school leaders may have to accept a lower quality decision rather than imposing controls that would undercut the restructuring process. Lower quality decisions may prove successful in the long run, however, due to the commitment of those involved in the decision process to make them work.

Many current school leaders will lack the attitudes or belief systems to support an enlarged role for teachers, students and the community. Some of these leaders are so conditioned by the bureaucratic system of rules and compliance that they may be hampered in enlarging options and opportunities for participation. It may not be that they think of an opportunity for participation and reject it so much as they never even consider the possibility.

Organizational cultures are highly resistant to change. Thus, the administrator must not be discouraged if progress is slow, particularly at first. It is critical, therefore, that the superintendent be extraordinarily clear about restructuring the rationale and the bureaucratic manifestations that seem so natural and necessary that no one even thinks to question them.

Synthesis of Research on Restructuring

The parameters of restructuring have attracted the attention of scholars. Sashkin [19] holds that four areas are involved: setting goals, making decisions, solving problems, and planning and carrying out organizational change. Duttweiler [20] has asserted that restructuring involves the following elements: principals as chief executive officers; realignment of salary schedules to shrink the income variance between central office personnel and principals and also between that of principals and teachers; a realignment of responsibilities to include more building level authority for curriculum, the technology of teaching and learning, acquisition of materials and the use of facilities and equipment, allocation of personnel, time, and money; and changing the role of central office personnel, from directing and monitoring compliance with central office programs to supporting school initiatives.

Decision-Making Authority

Decision-making authority is a key change in the restructured organization. Typically, discretion is permitted in three areas: budget, staffing, and curriculum [21]. To that list, Marburger [22] would add establishing school priorities and assessing the effectiveness of school programs. Staff development has been cited by Sanders and Wood [23] as an additional decision area delegated to the local site. Some schools have chosen to involve parents and teachers more deeply by developing school site councils with specified areas in which they can make decisions and others in which they can only make recommendations to the district board and/or apply for waivers [24].

In addition to decision-making authority in the areas above, districts are beginning to move on to allow decisions in such areas as ungraded classes, advanced uses of technology, and school-within-a-school arrangements. Some of these decisions impact on districtwide policy such as calendars, standards for promotion, and scheduling. School districts usually handle these needs by means of waivers from district policy [25]. Teachers are typically highly satisfied as they gain more opportunities to make decisions [26]. Research suggests that as teachers gain more decision-making authority, not only are they more satisfied, but they better meet the needs of their students [27].

Cautions in Restructuring

While there are decided benefits to restructuring, there are caveats to be observed as well. At its worst, restructuring can represent a power struggle between administrators, teachers, and parents [28]. Principals may not be clear as to what decisions they should make and which should be made in consultation with teachers [29]. Related to this, the central office may struggle with its role relative to the individual schools. While conflict with unions over union-negotiated prerogatives represents a possible roadblock to restructuring, this has not proven to be the case [30-33]. Even though participation in decision making is the centerpiece of restructuring, David [34] found that at the time of her research, the actual decision areas were rather limited with some marginal choices about staffing, a small discretionary budget for materials or staff development, a mechanism for teachers to be involved in certain decisions, an annual performance report, and a role for parents. Even within these restricted areas for change, researchers reported increases in teacher satisfaction and commitment [35,36].

Aspects of Restructuring

Several researchers have commented on the various aspects of restructuring. Cohen [37] of the National Governor's Association has identified five areas as the primary targets of restructuring:

- building bridges between schools and other service providers for students
- revamping curriculum and instruction to foster higher-order thinking in all students
- expanding school-based decision making

- rethinking the traditional roles of teachers and administrators
- making accountability systems more flexible

Cawelti [38] has noted seven key elements in restructuring:

- various degrees of site-based budgeting, affording alternative uses of resources
- a team operation affording groups (the opportunity) to expand the basis of decision making
- school-site advisory committees with key roles for parents at the high school level
- increased authority for selecting personnel who are assigned to the school
- the ability to modify the school's curriculum to better serve students
- clear processes for seeking waivers from local or state regulations that restrict the flexibility of local staffs
- an expectation for an annual report on progress and school improvement

Toward Educational Recovery

Restructuring is a formidable task, as can be seen from the reviews above. Efforts to restructure may even appear hopeless. Superintendents and their top aides, those who would be expected to provide the leadership, may not have the skills that have been identified as critical. Teachers, board members, and community members may be skeptical. Few can be expected to have the sensitivity to bureaucratic tendencies that may re-enter the organization and blunt the impact of restructuring because these tendencies will seem so necessary and, naturally, so familiar. In view of Goodlad's comment that few schools are actually restructuring, the task may seem impossible. A further concern may be that there does not seem to be any way to make a test run by trying out a few aspects or by starting with just one school. Systems theory tells us that a change in one part of the system necessarily impacts on all the other parts, thus once restructuring is introduced, a number of other changes either will be required, or will seem so necessary that to resist them would appear obstructionist.

These very real concerns must be balanced by the fact that educational recovery under bureaucratic organizational designs has not occurred. As effective as bureaucratic structures have been in the past in accomplishing educational goals, they do not meet current conditions. Restructuring is not experimental; it is already occurring in business and industry. Skills can be learned. Skeptics can be educated and won over. Multiple changes can be managed as time use shifts from the bureaucratic roles of directing and monitoring for compliance to collaborating and coordinating. As subordinates become empowered, the superintendent discovers that the former subordinates have become vested in the organization and are now, in effect, associates and assistants rather than subordinates who have to be monitored. Leaders in business and industry can be a valuable source of guidance during the implementation phase. Networking with like-minded school leaders can provide support and ideas.

Educational recovery will come. Today's school leaders are the best ones to lead this recovery. They have a wealth of valuable experience that, under organizational conditions fostering creativity and entrepreneurship, will produce the kind of improved educational opportunity business leaders are demanding, the public is expecting, politicians are promising, and children are deserving.

Troubleshooting

Each Troubleshooting section will pose a series of questions that focus on an understanding of the concepts presented in that chapter. This is the purpose of the Troubleshooting section, for it is absolutely essential that the leader of restructuring have a firm grasp of the concepts treated as they move into the uncharted waters of restructuring.

I'm still not clear why I couldn't just pilot this in one school, see how it goes, work out the bugs, and then implement it on a districtwide basis.

While this could possibly work, there are several problems with this approach. First, this approach does not require any changed behavior on the part of central office personnel. They can treat the pilot school as an aberration and continue their work as usual. Even if successful, there is no guarantee that the pilot project would spread to other schools smoothly. Others could point to the special aspects of the faculty or students at that school and claim that it would not work at their schools. Further, systems theory tells us that you can't make changes in one part of the system without affecting all the other parts of the system. Third, you are asking the faculty in the pilot school to engage in a considerable investment of time, energy, and professional expertise without any assurance that their efforts will be rewarded.

Restructuring is a long-term process. Since the point is to change the culture of the organization, the process can take from three to five years. Such an extended pilot would doubtless wear on the pilot personnel, and it is not clear that the culture of one school in a district can be changed if the rest of the district personnel continue to be rewarded for conventional behavior. But even if schools become more effective when restructured, success in one school will not necessarily provide helpful guidance for restructuring in the other schools, which may have an entirely different culture, history, student body, and parent group.

All of these reasons notwithstanding, local conditions might require a phase in. For example, some principals may be nearing retirement and thus may be unable to make the necessary shift in beliefs and practices. Other principals may be good followers once models are established in the district, but incapable of innovating with the first group. Still another group of principals might by many criteria seem to be leading a very successful school under conventional practice, where the potential loss could be greater than the projected gains. In fact, larger districts have generally phased in restructuring (Santa Fe, Baton Rouge, Miami-Dade) for a variety of reasons. If you chose to phase in restructuring, the following guidelines should help.

- Do not treat the early restructuring schools as pilots in the sense that, "If it doesn't work out, we'll discontinue it." Rather, make it clear that these schools are the vanguard and all schools in the district will be expected to move in that direction.
- Provide rewards, incentives, and recognition for the restructuring schools.
- Back the restructuring schools when the trouble comes as it most certainly will.
- Keep the board, professional staff, and community vision focused on preparing students for the 21st century. It is simply not enough that schools do well by current minimum competency standards.
- Set a timetable for the phase-in of additional schools. A plan is suggested in Chapter 6.

I'm still not sure I'm clear on the difference between site-based management, decentralization, and restructuring. Aren't they just different words for essentially the same thing?

No, they are not at all the same thing. Site-based management gives some authority to the individual building to make decisions on certain matters. However, there is no challenge to the basic bureaucratic assumptions. That is, the principal still can function as a director rather than a coordinator. While the principal's role with respect to teachers could change a great deal, if there is no expectation from the central office to substantially change the culture of the school, you are likely to witness a "site-based school" that differs little in operation or results from your schools currently.

Decentralization was popular in the late 1960s in large districts. This movement involved the creation of several zones which in effect operated as autonomous units within the larger school district. However, just as in site-based management, the basic bureaucratic assumptions remained in place and little improvement in student achievement was noted. In contrast to these two, restructuring requires a change in the basic operational assumptions of the organization; it requires a change in the culture of the organization; it requires shared decision making and collaboration. As a final distinction, decentralization and site-based management can be implemented over a summer; restructuring will take from three to five years.

You keep talking about how bad bureaucratic organization is. What exactly is wrong with it?

In some areas, bureaucratic organization has made and will continue to make important contributions to organizational goals. The problem is that by their very nature, bureaucracies emphasize control—rules have to be made, they have to be followed, there have to be rewards for those who follow the rules, and penalties for those who do not follow the rules. This may seem quite reasonable and logical, and some would say that this is the only way organizations could operate without complete chaos. As long as the work force is compliant, relatively naive, and relatively untrained, as long as the end goal is a standard product, and as long as the raw material (students) is relatively uniform, the bureaucratic organization works well. For a good part of the 20th century these assumptions have been reasonably accurate for education in America.

Now, however, conditions have changed. Teachers are far better educated than ever before. With this higher level of education, and with related factors such as the increasing power of minority groups, has come a rise in independence of thought and action. Students come to schools with a bewildering variety of backgrounds and attitudes. Parents are far more inclined to be vocal and critical about the schools, and far more interested in making choices in all areas of their lives. Goals that will prepare students for success in the 21st century tend to be less concrete, and less subject to verification by machine-scored standardized tests than those of the 20th century (problem solving, working as team members vs. picking out the best title for a sample paragraph, a typical exercise in standardized tests).

The successful organization of the 21st century will be more flexible, will rely more on the entrepreneurial activities of a highly educated work force, will develop more adaptable forms of accountability and will rely more on team decisions and input from its clientele. Organizations must be more flexible because the pace of change is accelerating so rapidly, a concept first popularized by Toffler in *Future Shock* [39]. Thus, because the goals have changed, the teaching force has changed, the students have changed, and the pace of change has changed, the old bureaucratic organizational principles are no longer sufficient.

As you have described it, restructuring must be implemented all at once, most of my subordinates will not have the necessary skills, and much of my community and even the board and teachers may not see the need for such a radical change. It's beginning to look too difficult to me. I'm beginning to think that I will just introduce a few changes, tell others that we are beginning the restructuring process, and hope that this whole thing blows over.

Doubtless a number of superintendents will follow this approach. However, we do not believe that restructuring is a bandwagon. We do not believe it will blow over. We see it as the culmination of changes that have been occurring over the past twenty-five years. During that time we have observed the empowerment of various racial groups and women. We have seen business become far more consumer-oriented, offering far more choices to customers. We are witnessing the collapse of bureaucratic, top-down, centralized planning in the Eastern European countries and the shift to a competitive, market-driven economy, as communist government after communist government falls. We hear the world's top communist leader, Mikhail Gorbachev, extol perestroika, e.g. restructuring, which is designed to introduce more competition and promote more entrepreneurial commitment and creativity in the Soviet work force. We believe that the principles represented by restructuring are global and, ultimately, irresistible.

Implementation Checklist

_____ 1. All professional staff know and can explain to parents and the community at large the reasons why the bureaucratic system is no longer working.

_____ 2. All professional staff know and can explain to parents and the community at large the reasons why restructuring promises dramatic improvements in preparing students for the 21st century.

_____ 3. Those responsible for leading restructuring implementation (principals, lead teachers, parent leaders) are aware of the energy and persistence necessary to make the fundamental changes required and are committed to it.

_____ 4. A thorough review of all procedures has been conducted to eliminate those that foster bureaucratic practices such as creating paper trails, emphasizing compliance, making decisions on the basis of voting, and so forth.

_____ 5. Procedures have been put into place that foster restructuring such as decision making by consensus, an emphasis on effectiveness rather than efficiency, power based on competence rather than position, and so forth.

_____ 6. A watchdog group has been appointed to alert decision makers to bureaucratic practices that might creep back into the system (or never be fully purged).

_____ 7. Variation from school to school is expected and encouraged by the central office.

_____ 8. The role of the central office has shifted from that of monitoring for compliance and being the source of all ideas for improvement to acting as a support group to aid schools in their change initiatives.

_____ 9. Principals have been paired to observe each other on a periodic basis and offer feedback on their interactions with staff, students, and parents.

_____ 10. Outcome expectations on a wide range of student goals for the 21st century have been established, but school sites are expected to devise their own initiatives for achieving those outcome expectations.

_____ 11. Organizational administrators have committed themselves to the belief that leadership is widespread, not limited to the formal leaders.

_____ 12. Organizational members have confronted the "Cautions Regarding Restructuring" and have come to grips with these.

References

1. Olsen, L. 1988. "The Restructuring Puzzle," *Education Week* (November):7.

2. *The Texas Learning Technology Group.* 1989. Austin, TX: The Group.

3. Council of Chief State School Officers. 1989. *Success for All in a New Century.* Washington, D.C.: The Council.

4. Weber, M. 1946. "Bureaucracy," in *From Max Weber.* H. Gerth and C.W. Mills, eds. New York: Oxford Press, pp. 196-244.

5. Weick, K. 1976. "Educational Organizations as Loosely Coupled Systems," *Administrative Science Quarterly*, 21:1-19.

6. McNeil, L. 1986. *Contradictions of Control.* London: Rautledge and Kagan Paul.

7. Sizer, T. 1986. *Perspectives on Education.* Videotape. Bloomington, IN: Phi Delta Kappa.

8. Kanter, R. M. 1983. *The Change Masters.* New York: Simon and Schuster.

9. Kearns, D. 1988. "An Educational Recovery Plan for America," *Phi Delta Kappan*, 69:565-575.

10. Shanker, A. "Professionalizing Teachers," Speech at the *Annual Conference of the National Council of States on Inservice Education, New Orleans, November 1987.*

11. Task Force on Teaching as a Profession of the Carnegie Forum on Education and the Economy. 1986. *A Nation Prepared: Teachers for the 21st Century.* New York: Carnegie Corporation.

12. Drucker, P. 1988. "The Coming of the New Organization," *Harvard Business Review*, 66:45-53.

13. O'Toole, J. 1985. *Vanguard Management.* Garden City, NY: Doubleday.

14. Reich, R. B. 1987. "Entrepreneurship Reconsidered: The Team as Hero," *Harvard Business Review*, 65:80-81.

15. Shulman, L. 1987. "Assessment for Teaching: An Initiative for the Profession," *Phi Delta Kappan*, 69:38-44.

16. Sergiovanni, T. and R. Starratt. 1988. *Supervision: Human Perspectives, 4th Edition.* New York: McGraw-Hill.

17. Burns, J. M. 1978. *Leadership.* New York: Harper and Row.

18. Pipho, C. 1989. "Objects in This Mirror May Be Closer Than They Appear," *Phi Delta Kappan*, 71:262-263.

19. Sashkin, M. 1986. "Participative Management Remains an Ethical Imperative," *Organizational Dynamics*, 14:62-75.

20. Duttweiler, P. C. 1989. "A Look at School Based Management," *Insights* (January):1-4.

21. Clunne, W. H. and P. A. White. 1988. *School Based Management: Institutional Variation, Implementation, and Issues for Further Research.* Madison, WI: Center for Policy Research in Education.

22. Marburger, C. 1985. *One School at a Time.* Columbia, MD: The National Committee for Citizens in Education.

23. Sanders, W. L. and F. Wood. 1989. "A Model for Shared Leadership," *Texas Study of Secondary Education Research Journal*, (45):35-37.

24. Marburger, loc. cit.

25. David, J. 1989. "Synthesis of Research on School Based Management," *Educational Leadership*, 47:45-53.

26. Clune and White, loc. cit.

27. Knight, P. 1984. "The Practice of School Based Curriculum Development," *Journal of Curriculum Studies*, 7:37-48.

28. White, P. A. 1988. *Resource Materials on School Based Management*. New Brunswick, NJ: Center for Policy Research in Education, Rutgers University.

29. Kennison, R. Personal communication with the superintendent (October 24, 1988).

30. Gomez, J. J. 1989. "The Path to School Based Management Isn't Smooth, but We're Scaling the Obstacles One by One," *The American School Board Journal*, 176:20-22.

31. McWalters, P. 1988. "New Realities Call for New Rules," *The School Administrator,* 8:13-16.

32. Payzant, T. W. 1989. "To Restructure Schools, We've Changed the Way the Bureaucracy Works," *The American School Board Journal*, 176:19-20.

33. Urbanski, A. 1988. "The Rochester Contract: A Status Report," *Educational Leadership*, 46:48-52.

34. David, loc. cit.

35. Harrison, C. R., J. P. Killion, and J. E. Mitchell. 1989. "Site Based Management: The Realities of Implementation," *Educational Leadership*, 47:55-58.

36. Scarr, L. E. 1988. "Lake Washington's Master Plan—A System for Growth," *Educational Leadership*, 46:13-16.

37. Cohen, M. "Lessons from Restructuring Pilots," Speech at the *Annual Convention of the Association for Supervision and Curriculum Development, Orlando, FL, March 1989.*

38. Cawelti, G. 1989. "Key Elements of Site Based Management," *Educational Leadership,* 47:46.

39. Toffler, A. 1971. *Future Shock*. New York: Bantam Books.

② Leaders for Restructuring

Traditional Views of Leadership

Characteristics of the traditional, bureaucratic organization were reviewed in Chapter 1. Leaders of such organizations are expected to carry out the rules and policies of the organization in the most efficient and effective manner possible. Further, they are expected to recommend rule changes that will enable the organization to operate in a more efficient and effective manner. A frequently encountered acronym to describe the functions of the traditional leader is POSDCORB—Planning, Organizing, Staffing, Developing, Coordinating, Reporting, and Budgeting.

While these roles are important to the maintenance of the organization, they do not look beyond the current system to what might be. Under this view, problems are considered to be a minor flaw in an otherwise satisfactory system; consequently, the role of the leader becomes that of changing a part of the system to solve the problem. This approach can be quite effective if the changes in society are quite slow or if there is little expectation that the organization will be affected by those changes. Neither of these assumptions are accurate currently; thus, the POSDCORB approach, while including necessary maintenance responsibilities, is not sufficient.

Another traditional approach is to characterize the leadership function in terms of responsibilities—executive, manager, public relations, and educator [1]. In this framework, the executive is considered the boss, the dispenser of rewards and punishments and as policy advisor/interpreter of board policy. As manager, the leader has responsibilities in the areas of finance, school facilities, personnel, and auxiliary services. In the public relations role, the leader is seen as a visible spokesperson to the community on educational matters. As educator, the leader is expected to assist in the selection of educational objectives and to implement economically the most effective programs. Similar to the POSDCORB analysis, this view presents

21

programs. Similar to the POSDCORB analysis, this view presents maintenance as the prevailing leadership function that, again, has been an acceptable approach in the past.

Conventional Views of Leadership

Conventional views of school leadership are reflected in a number of the skills lists developed by various professional organizations.

Skills for Successful School Leaders [2]

- designing, implementing, and evaluating the school climate
- building support for schools
- developing school curriculum
- instructional management
- staff evaluation
- staff development
- allocating resources
- educational research, evaluation, and planning

Performance-Based Preparation for Principals [3]

- problem analysis
- judgement (to include "identifying educational needs and setting priorities")
- organizational ability
- decisiveness
- leadership (to include "getting others involved in solving problems")
- sensitivity (to include "skill in resolving conflicts")
- stress tolerance
- oral communication
- written communication
- range of interests
- personal motivation
- educational values (to include "possession of a well-reasoned educational philosophy")

Emergent Views of Leadership

Emergent views of leadership see leaders less in terms of skills (current leadership views) and functions (traditional leadership views) and more as human resource developers. Thus, for example,

Batten [4] describes leadership by expectations. He contrasts this with traditional management in that traditional managers tell, push, and drive whereas emergent leadership gets commitment, expects the best from each person, takes the time to sit down and learn the drives and ambitions of each team member, develops with them goals they can reach if they stretch, holds them accountable for results (without insisting that they follow a company-approved process for obtaining those results), and rewards them for performance that contributes to organizational goals. Calling this leader orientation "empowerment," Bennis and Nanus [5] write that empowerment involves neither the leader giving power away, nor subordinates constantly challenging leaders. Rather, power becomes a unit of exchange in which the leader empowers and by that act gains power to lead still further. Similarly to Batten, Bennis and Nanus say that leaders should pull, not push.

The Power of Vision

How exactly do leaders change from pushing to pulling? Bennis and Nanus tell of the compelling power of vision, a power that pulls. Vision, they relate, creates focus. This focus leads to an agenda and intensity on the part of the leader. Vision, coupled with the commitment and intensity it generates, is magnetic. Bennis and Nanus report that the leaders in their study communicated their vision through metaphors. A metaphor for the leader of a bureaucratic organization might be the engineer on a train going straight down the tracks—everything follows in an orderly way. By contrast, a metaphor for the leader of a restructured organization might be that of one trying to induce an amoeba to move in a certain direction. One would push here, pull there, and with cooperation from the amoeba, the whole would move generally in the desired direction [6]. Metaphors help organizational members focus on what is important in the organization. A powerful metaphor that captures the essence of the vision gives subordinates a sense that the organization is going somewhere, and motivates them to commit their energy, creativity, and attention.

Organizations for Pull Leadership

As the vision is being clearly established in the minds of the organizational members, the leader must be creating the organization that will foster "pull" leadership. Kanter [7] has described such organizations. The organization itself is integrated, not segmented into neat compartments, and job descriptions tend to be broad. Thus, a certain tolerance for ambiguity is required of the leader. This ambiguous organization, in combination with a powerful vision as described by Bennis and Nanus, permits subordinates to test possibilities and alternatives. Kanter continues by detailing the process by which subordinates secure the power to test their ideas—a process called securing "buy-in." Buy-in consists of four steps: preselling (seeking the support of other key personnel), tin-cupping (seeking support for the idea, either monetary or official), sanity-checking (testing the feasibility of the idea with an older, more experienced colleague), and push-back (a key supporter suggests that he is pulling out—this acts as another sanity-check to test the commitment of the team that is being formed).

Kanter is describing a process of empowerment. Power is not given. Rather, the leader creates a system by which power may be gained by the subordinate but with sufficient checks to insure the soundness of the concept and the commitment of the individual to carry it out. As widespread understanding of this process of power acquisition is developed by the subordinates, the leader must make sure that power resources (information, resources, and support) are available at the building level. With a clearly communicated vision and an organization that permits subordinates to gain power, the leader is now in a position to exercise "pull" rather than "push" leadership if the subordinates are motivated to try out their ideas.

Transactional and Transformational Motivation

Burns [8] has described two kinds of motivational drives that leaders tap—transactional and transformational. Transactional motivation is the exchange of valued things, work in exchange for salary, for example. Other examples of traditionally used transactional motivation devices would be the use of titles, special services, compensatory time, favored room assignments or schedules, and so forth. Sergiovanni and Starratt [9] have noted that such a motivational approach leads subordinates to engage in participation investment—a day's work for a day's pay. While this motivational approach may have been effective in traditional organizations, it will not produce the level of employee commitment and creativity required to achieve success in today's society. Sergiovanni [10] and others have described another powerful motivational approach, transformational motivation.

Burns [11] was the first to describe the power of transformational motivation. He defined it as the leader engaging with others in such a way that both leader and subordinate are raised to higher levels of motivation and morality. He goes on to note that whereas the purposes of the leader and the led in transactional motivation begin and remain separate (the leader wants the work done; the worker wants the salary), in transformational motivation, the purposes of the leader and the subordinate become fused. The leader is then in a position to pull rather than push. But how is the leader able to tap the transformational motivational drive?

Moral Values and Vanguard Leadership

O'Toole [12] has termed the new leadership "vanguard leadership." According to O'Toole, vanguard leaders are characterized by balance, integration, harmony, coherence, and justice. When faced with a decision, they are guided by their commitment to do the right thing for their divergent constituencies—the customers, the owners of stock, the employees, and the communities in which their companies are located. A very important point is that they are not just guided by this principle when things are going well; they follow this principle when there are problems in the economy, when they are facing heavy competition, when they are being criticized by Wall Street. O'Toole even recounts an occasion in which the manager of a plant that had achieved a high level of productivity was fired because he had achieved the productivity level by pushing the employees to unreasonable limits.

By comparison, can we imagine any situation in which a principal would get fired in a school that had achieved high test scores? The presumption would be that whatever he was doing must be the right thing to do because he was getting results. O'Toole suggests that the reason his vanguard leaders were able to make decisions based on high moral values is that they kept long-term results in mind. They reason that if one of their constituencies feels unfairly treated, that group will eventually reduce its level of commitment and productivity and the level of quality will soon follow. This is not, however, a "management philosophy." Rather, it is a deep commitment to principle, to enduring values, to people—all the people served by the organization.

Others have commented on this deep commitment to moral values as well. Sergiovanni [13] has described value-added leadership. In contrast to conventional leadership, value-added leadership emphasizes leadership rather than management; enhancing meaning rather than manipulating situations; enabling subordinates rather than giving directions; building an accountability system rather than installing a monitoring system; developing collegiality rather than congeniality; and leading with passion rather than calculation. These changes in leadership must be practiced with high moral integrity, however, to be effective. According to Sergiovanni, leadership is an offer to control. The follower accepts this offer with the understanding that this control will not be exploited. Sergiovanni concludes that the test of leadership is whether the follower and the organization are enhanced or diminished by the leader's actions.

In his study of a Lighthouse Principal, Reavis [14] found that the principal was able to turn many issues into moral issues; then he was able to choose the appropriate action and convince others to support him. For example, proper teacher attire became for this principal an issue in modeling professional dress for students who might not otherwise have this example—he made no reference to dress codes, district policy, and so forth. The teacher came to see her selection of attire as an educational issue, not as a compliance issue. In this light, the teacher agreed to a change in attire. On another occasion, the cafeteria manager wanted to change the procedure by which the free or reduced price lunches were accounted for. Rather than question her about possible complications for himself or problems in interfacing with the central office accounting, he asked her about the impact on the students—would the proposed process increase or diminish their self-esteem?—thus making it a moral rather than a management issue.

Peters and Austin [15] stress the centrality of concern for people in their study of excellent companies. They summarize their findings by noting that the leaders exhibit a bone-deep commitment to everyone in the organization. Note that this commitment is not contingent on being earned—it is unconditional. If you are in the company, you are valued—period.

Returning to O'Toole's vanguard managers, in addition to the moral basis of leadership and treating all of their constituencies fairly, the vanguard leaders stress being the best at everything their organization attempts. Simply stated, they stress quality. It is one thing to state that high quality is an organizational value; it is quite another to make it a part of the culture of the organization. The vanguard leaders achieve this emphasis by a continual stress on quality—rewarding it, exhibiting it, and supporting those who hold out for it. Quality has to become one of the core values if employees are to develop pride in the organization. Pride, in turn, is the ultimate guardian of quality.

A final characteristic O'Toole notes is that these leaders stress continuous learning. They are learners themselves, and they expect their organizational members to be learners as well. They are constantly bringing new ideas, distributing information, seeking out development opportunities for their subordinates, and so forth. Further, these leaders build a culture in which ideas are expected to be tried out, not merely contemplated as "interesting." To foster risk-taking, leaders communicate that mistakes are to be expected.

Leader Behaviors/Values That Foster Restructuring

In the section above on conventional views of leadership, a summary of the recommendations of several professional groups for school principals or superintendents was presented. The problem with those lists is not that they are bad so much as that they do not anticipate building the school organizations of the future. At best they anticipate modest improvements of current practice following conventional organizational understandings. Indeed, it is difficult to specify the behaviors and values needed for restructuring because so few school districts are actually engaged in it. Reavis [15], however, has surveyed a number of districts known to be engaging in restructuring and has gained an understanding of the needed behaviors as reported by those implementing restructuring. In developing the questionnaire, he reviewed lists of educational leader skills published by professional organizations similar to the ones listed in the section on conventional views of leadership. This list was then circulated to the leaders of twenty-five school districts known to be restructuring. Responses were received from the leaders of seventeen districts. Of the forty-four items on the list, the highest nine are reported below.

Knowledge of Change Management

This was by far the highest rated requirement for school restructuring. The stages of change are identification of a problem or need, selection of a response, gathering of information, preparation, initiation, development, adoption, implementation, support, evaluation, and revision. Typically, however, many change initiatives have focused on one intervention, such as improving the reading program, rather than on holistic change. The result has frequently been a modest or no improvement in outcome. Restructuring requires a holistic approach to change. That is, a total plan for change must be developed involving all aspects of the organization—budget, personnel, curriculum, instruction, decision making, culture, and so forth.

Further, the community and the board must be prepared for the changes and the inevitable problems that will surface any time change is initiated. For example, staff may become discouraged and student achievement may actually decrease while professional staff are learning their new roles. The best preparation in change management is to thoroughly prepare key staff in the process, to establish the need with staff and the public, and to have a comprehensive plan. Those who initiate change are sometimes guilty of underestimating the difficulty of genuine change and the persistence that will be required to sustain change once it is initiated. Old habits creep in, people get tired, resistance forms, the benefits are distant, and leaders sometimes settle for the appearance of change rather than for real, fundamental change.

Collaborative Leadership Style

For many leaders this will be both uncomfortable and fear-inducing. To collaborate with others and act on their recommendations when these recommendations may go against one's own inclination takes a high degree of trust and risk-tolerance. This concern can be diminished somewhat by informing the board and public of the change in decision-making processes and the reasons for the change (the reasons for change from the bureaucratic structure have been discussed in Chapter 1). The steps in collaboration will be discussed in Chapter 3.

Team Building

There is a substantial difference between a group and a team. A group can be any assembly of people. By contrast, a team shares a commitment, a purpose, as well as a sense of trust, caring, and appreciation for one another. Consider the difference between a football *team* and a football *group*. Whereas a bureaucracy can run very well with groups of people, a restructured organization must have a leader who can build teams. Team building will be developed in Chapter 3.

Educational Values

Leaders of bureaucratic organizations are committed to a variety of values—fiscal responsibility, political survival, compliance with regulations, good publicity, winning athletic teams, and so forth. Leaders of restructured organizations are driven by the central importance of education, not just any education, but the best—that which will serve all students well. Students and education provide the spur that charges their persistence in the very difficult task of change. Their educational values are expressed in short, pithy statements such as "Success for every child," "Every kid a winner," and "All children can learn." They see education as the only ticket out for many of their students, and they are driven by the determination to make that education accessible to all.

High Moral Purpose/Sense of Purpose

This factor has already been considered in this chapter. Leaders of restructured schools see their mission as much higher than merely doing a job well. They are on a crusade. They are not dull or tedious, but they do see the import of their leadership far beyond "running a tight ship." They are concerned with the direction of the ship, the purpose of the voyage. As has already been stated, it is this high moral purpose that sustains their efforts in difficult times, and proves so highly motivating to their subordinates.

Knowledge of Curriculum and Instruction

In the past a familiar cliché has held that the primary job of a school administrator was to be an instructional leader. Chiefly, this has consisted of ceremonial activities. For the most part, instructional leadership was left up to department chairs or individual teachers. Leaders of restructured organizations have a solid working knowledge of curriculum and instruction and a clear vision of what education is and isn't. While they work collaboratively with other leaders in the organization, they work as equals, not as rubber stamps. They view the curriculum holistically and see their role as orchestrating an educational milieu, not merely adding a course here, a program there. Their vision is focused on the future. They know that we have entered the Information Age and that the jobs of the future are going to involve the processing of information to solve problems. A more detailed account of the demands of a curriculum for the 21st century will be presented in Chapter 4.

A Sound, Well-Reasoned Philosophy

Because leaders of restructuring are venturing out on relatively uncharted waters, they must have a sure sense of their purpose. It is this sense of purpose that will guide them through the often confusing, conflicting paradoxes that will confront them in the process of fundamental change. Someone has described the process of restructuring as trying to convert a steam locomotive to diesel while the locomotive is going down the tracks.

Bennis [16] lists four factors that characterize leaders who inspire trust in their subordinates:

- Constancy—even when they experience surprises themselves, they smooth them out for their subordinates.
- Congruity—the theories they promote are the theories they live out.
- Reliability—they are there when they are needed; they support their subordinates.
- Integrity—they honor their commitments and promises.

In order for a leader to exhibit these he must have a sound personal, educational, and organizational philosophy. Elements of a sound organizational philosophy have been introduced in Chapter 1. Elements of an educational philosophy for restructuring will be presented in Chapter 4. The personal philosophy that sustains leaders during restructuring is a deep conviction of the importance of education in the future of the individual child and a conviction that every child can learn [17].

Knowledge of Climate/Culture and How to Change/Shape These

"Climate" is the way members of an organization feel about that organization. "Culture" refers to the understood rules about how things work in the organization and is transferred by traditions, celebrations, rituals, and stories about heroes of the organization. Thus, a subordinate might feel that his ideas are valued in the organization (climate); an annual ritual might be the celebration of technological breakthroughs that are the result of subordinate ideas (culture).

A climate survey will give the leader the current perception of subordinates; to change that perception, culture must be altered. For example, if a climate survey revealed that organizational members felt decisions were made solely on the basis of convenience, or so as not to disturb power forces in the organization, or for budgetary reasons, the leader might wish to change the culture in order to change the climate. The leader could meet with key members of the organization and make a decision on another basis (on the basis of research, for example, or on the basis of what is best for children), articulate this to the organizational members, model this behavior himself, recognize others who practice this behavior, and make it a required part of all decision-making processes. Over time the climate of the organization would be altered to reflect the changed culture. A suggested instrument for identifying the climate of the organization is included in Appendix A.

Sensitivity

Sensitivity is defined as an awareness of the impact of one's behavior on others. This is an extremely important characteristic for leaders in restructuring organizations because the changes required are so contrary to conventional organizational practice that subordinates can be frequently confused or frustrated. Recognizing this and responding with empathy and support can be vital in keeping members of the organization committed to restructuring and confident in their changed roles.

ASCD Study of Crucial Skills for Facilitators of Restructuring

Saxl, Lieberman, and Miels[18] have developed a training program for ASCD based on their study of seventeen successful facilitators in the school change process (although not necessarily in restructuring). The training program contains the following six modules:

(1) *Trust and rapport building*—This involves connecting quickly and easily with people and building a safe, non-threatening environment that supports risk-taking and experimentation.

(2) *Organizational diagnosis*—This is based on the leader's understanding of organizational theory (see Chapter 1) and on his vision of the organization that will foster restructuring. A climate survey (Appendix B) is a good way to begin the diagnosis.

(3) *Dealing with the improvement process*—This revolves around three skills: collaboration (helping people work together productively on a collegial basis), conflict management (helping people with differing viewpoints to deal with these constructively), and confrontation (being able to be frank about concerns, to "tell it like it is").

(4) *Resource utilization*—Get ideas and materials together with people who can utilize them, including trips to other sites that are using the materials or processes.

(5) *Managing the work of improvement teams*—Include skills of time management and organization and the commitment to "keep things moving."

(6) *Building the capacity to continue*—Facilitators must empower others to continue when the facilitator is not present. This entails building an understanding of the process being used (collaboration, for example) as well as using the process at the time.

While these skills were identified as crucial for facilitators in school change processes, many of them should prove useful to leaders of restructuring as well. Specifically, skills (1), (2), and (3) track very closely with those found by Reavis in his survey above.

Competencies of Leaders for Restructuring

A LEAD Restructuring Study Group Seminar has identified competencies necessary for leaders carrying out restructuring [19]. It is significant that this group noted that all participants in restructuring—superintendents, principals, and teachers would need training in skills for restructuring. Otherwise, those leading restructuring would be set up for frustration and burnout.

(1) *Visionary leadership*—This would include the subskills of understanding change and the change process, analyzing, conceptualizing an improved state of the organization, relating operational elements (budget and resource management) to student learning, and encouraging creativity.

(2) *Cultural leadership*—Included in cultural leadership are the skills of varying leadership according to the particular situation, recognizing the organizational culture and the norms that the culture promotes, shaping norms that support reflective and collegial practice, and extinguishing norms that subvert organizational vision.

(3) *Symbolic leadership*—This would include promoting public relations, knowing how to "walk your talk," conveying importance through attention, visibility, and passion, and understanding motivation.

(4) *Instructional leadership*—The aspects of this skill would be understanding curriculum alignment and integration, understanding the relationships among the factors that promote student learning, using research data to improve practice, applying technology, and using evaluation data to improve performance.

(5) *Reflective practice*—This included giving and receiving specific performance feedback, as well as considering past and current actions in light of new information and with a view toward improved practice.

(6) *Creating work force norms that support collegiality*—The sub-skills in this category included skill in using the group process, networking, team-building, facilitating, modeling, trust-building, and using collaborative processes.

(7) *Creating leadership density*—This included the skills of recognizing leadership talent and nurturing and developing leadership growth.

(8) *Identifying leverage points*—This final skill included the sub-skills of recognizing windows of opportunity and capitalizing on leverage to improve student learning.

New Roles for New Leaders

A comparison of the skills for restructuring and the conventional leadership skills listed above is instructive. The words "values," "culture," "collaboration," "change management," "team-building," "instructional leadership," and "trust" keep appearing on the lists of skills for restructuring. All of these words convey a vision of a leader who is very comfortable in working with others on an equal basis. Further, they convey an image of a leader who can tolerate a certain amount of ambiguity. They also suggest a leader who is willing to take calculated risks, that is, who can embark on a process without knowing exactly how it may change as it unfolds. In a sense, these words convey a different vision of leadership entirely. Rather than think in terms of "a leader," we perhaps need to think in terms of "leaders." This would be more in line with the position of Burns [20] who wrote of the infinite depth of leadership behind the recognized leader. A currently popular phrase is that those who are doing the job know best how to do it. With this insight on the depth of leadership, those doing the job must be included in the decision-making loop; in a sense, every member of the organization is a leader.

While the above listed roles for leaders of restructured organizations are the key roles for restructuring, they do not represent the only roles required of the leader of a modern organization. Bradford and Cohen [21] have described the "manager as developer." They note that the outdated image of a leader is that of a hero, doing all the work, making all the decisions himself. For certain personality types this image is very seductive and such individuals can be very effective in organizational accomplishment. Most modern organizations, however, will be better served by the manager as developer model of leadership.

Bradford and Cohen list three components of this leadership model: building a shared responsibility team (a group that makes the core decisions for the unit); providing for continuous development of individual skills; and determining and building a common organization vision. Of these three, the first step is the building of an organizational vision, which must reflect the core purpose of the organization, must be feasible and challenging, and must have a larger significance. If the subordinate is to participate fully in a shared responsibility team, he must be aided in developing his skills. Key skills for the leader in order that he may develop his subordinates include being able to communicate directly, looking beyond difficult personality characteristics to the causes of those characteristics, drawing subordinates close, giving behaviorally specific feedback, and genuinely caring about the development of his subordinates.

The third step, building the shared responsibility team, goes through several predictable stages. At first the participants will be cautious and will function only nominally as members of a team, or perhaps they will divide into subgroups. The next stage is likely to be confrontation. This can be very unnerving for the group leader (you), but it is a sign of growth of the group. The stage of shared responsibility is marked by open, supportive relationships, commitment to the vision of the organization, decisions by consensus, reciprocal relationships with the formal leader (members feel free to agree or disagree), and attention to the way the group is working. The building of the shared responsibility team is a powerful step in restructuring an organization and is discussed in detail in Chapter 3.

Yukl [22] has provided a list of the skills, detailed below, which the leader of a modern organization must possess. These are expected of both formal and informal leaders in the organization, but the formal leaders will model them to a high degree.

Maintaining Good Leader-Subordinate Relations

This includes cooperative relations with high levels of mutual trust and loyalty, considerate/supportive behavior demonstrated by being friendly, open, sympathetic, and helpful, as well as by treating subordinates fairly, showing respect, demonstrating concern for the needs of subordinates, and by helping them advance their careers. Further, subordinates expect the leader to provide recognition and equitable rewards, represent subordinate interests to superiors, and allow participation in decisions that affect the subordinates' interests. Personal skills that are helpful are those of tact and diplomacy, empathy for subordinates' needs and feelings, listening skills, social sensitivity, and counseling skills.

Maintaining Good Relationships with Peers and Superiors

This includes monitoring events in the organization, network building, and representing the organization in the larger community. There is a relationship between the upward influence of the leader and the influence he exerts with his subordinates. If he is unable to gain the necessary resources, protect subordinate interests, and gain approval for necessary changes from the board, state agencies, or other power sources, the leader is not likely to exert much influence with his subordinates.

Gathering and Using Information

This includes monitoring the internal and external environment, informing members of the organization and clarifying information. A large part of a leader's job is gathering, analyzing, and disseminating information; thus, cultivation of information sources both inside and outside the organization through face-to-face contact is an important aspect of the job.

Making Decisions

This includes analyzing problems, identifying causal patterns and trends, and forecasting likely outcomes of alternative decisions. Decision processes are usually characterized by more confusion, disorder and emotionality than is typically reported in the literature. Consequently, leaders must have self-confidence, stress-tolerance, and tolerance of ambiguity.

Motivating and Influencing Others

This includes possessing high self-confidence, a need for power, relevant expertise, political insight, and persuasive ability. Leaders inspire subordinates to commit to new objectives and strategies by modeling exemplary behavior, activating needs for achievement and power, and appealing to values such as "serving justice," "being the best," "finding the time" or "doing a noble deed."

Faced with the conventional demands for leadership cited by Yukl as well as the additional demands exerted by restructuring and the maintenance responsibilities of a manager, the leader might reasonably react by asking, "Where do I get the time?" Time for leadership in restructuring comes from several sources. First, the leader is freed from the monitoring and compliance duties associated with leadership in the bureaucratic model. These responsibilities take a substantial amount of time given the need to specify how activities are to be conducted, how records are to be maintained to create a paper trail, designing all of the processes and procedures that insure the system will work, answering questions about compliance and exceptions, and so forth. The leader will have been essentially freed from these activities because subordinates will have been empowered to act in the best interests of the children, and thus there is no need for much of the monitoring and directing activity that formerly took so much leadership time.

A second source of time is that the empowered subordinates are highly energized by the moral challenge of providing the best education possible for children and need little motivating; instead, they seek extra opportunities for service. Rather than spending time having to figure out ways around bureaucratic blocks, they find themselves in an enabling environment that makes their time more productive and satisfying. This leads to a third source of time-saving for the leader – fewer personnel problems. Satisfied subordinates find less to be disgruntled about. Needless to say, these savings do not occur overnight, and in the transition period the leader will have to work extended amounts of time. In the long run, however, the leader and his subordinates will find increasing amounts of their time spent in a manner that is more effective and satisfying, that is, keeping the organization on course, helping members continue to enlarge their understanding of how the restructured organization can help them to exercise their professional skills, focusing on producing results rather than meeting requirements, enlarging organizational and professional skills, and shaping instructional and curriculum responses to prepare children for the 21st century and a global economy.

Troubleshooting

I'm still not sure I understand the difference between my current leadership practices and leadership for restructuring. I hold meetings with my people. I tell them I want their best ideas. I encourage them to be innovative. I try to free them from as much red tape as possible. I encourage them to make decisions on their own. I think I listen to my people. I have asked them to work on public relations. I may have been practicing leadership for restructuring and not realized it!

The difference is not so much in kind, perhaps, as in emphasis. A good exercise might be to track how you are using your time. If you are like administrators in many bureaucratic organizations, your day is chopped up into brief conferences. What is the focus of these conferences? What goes on in the meetings you call? Below you will find a leadership test that juxtaposes conventional leadership and leadership for restructuring. This should help you to get a sense of the difference between conventional leadership and leadership for restructuring.

Restructuring Leadership Test

Questions

1. Are you a controller or a developer?

2. Do you trust your subordinates to make the right decision or do you need to have them run it by you for your approval?

3. Do you stress doing the right things, or do you stress doing things right?

4. When faced with an important decision, do you seek justification in policy or do you decide on the basis that it is in the best interests of the children?

5. If a subordinate comes to you with a question, do you give him an answer, or do you help him arrive at his own conclusion?

6. When you consider subordinates for promotion, do you select one who has shown initiative or do you select one who has a record of following policy and not rocking the boat?

7. Do you tend to rely on a small group for advice or do you include all concerned parties?

8. Do you rely on professional colleagues for ideas on school change or do you involve other interested parties such as businesses, parents, and community leaders?

9. Do you prefer to change one part of your organization, or are you willing to try to change a number of factors at once?

10. If things go wrong, do you take the blame yourself (even if you were only indirectly involved) or do you look for the guilty party?

Answers

1. The restructuring leader is a developer. Rather than exercise control, he develops the leadership capabilities in his subordinates. This is a critical behavior for leaders of restructuring for, by contrast, conventional leadership in a bureaucratic organization is founded on control. Most of the systems are designed for control.

2. Trust of one's subordinates is critical for developing leadership in one's subordinates. To be sure, the trust will be misplaced from time to time. Some, perhaps most, subordinates, trained in the bureaucratic tradition, may be uncomfortable with this trust and may even resent it. Rather than being responsible for results based on decisions and actions they have initiated, they may be more familiar with and comfortable with carrying out decisions made at another level. The leader in restructuring is required to install a new responsibility which may well be resisted.

3. In one sense this is a false dichotomy. Certainly one should stress doing things right as opposed to doing them wrong. The point of this question is that so often bureaucratic policy, rules, and traditions are the basis of judging the rightness of an action or decision. This basis must be shifted to a moral basis, to doing the right thing.

4. The rationale for this question is similar to that of Question #3. Policy has so often guided our sense of the proper action to take. If entrepreneurship is to be fostered in the organization, policy must become a less dominating factor. Much policy can be replaced with goals and parameters.

5. The restructuring leader will help the subordinate arrive at his own answer. The rationale for this answer is similar to the one for Question #1. As long as the leader gives the answer, he reinforces the dependency of the subordinate and the uniformity of the organization. Is this to say that the restructuring leader never answers a question? Certainly not. It is to say that the leader will carefully weigh each question to determine if it is, indeed, a closed question (i.e., having only one right answer) or if a variety of "right answers" are possible.

6. In evaluating subordinates for possible promotion, the restructuring leader will want to favor those who have shown initiative. These are the ones who have the personal confidence to assume more responsibility for decision making at the local building level and to nurture this same orientation in others.

7. Some leaders come to depend on a trusted group of peers or subordinates for most of their input on certain decisions. The restructuring leader will include all subordinates affected by the decision (or a representative group if the number of subordinates is large). The rationale for this answer is similar to the one for Question #2.

8. All interested parties should be included in the decision even though they may not have the professional expertise. The rationale for this answer is similar to the one for Question #2.

9. Most leaders are likely to answer that they have, in the past, attempted to change one part of the organization. If an organization is to be restructured, however, many of the main structures will have to be changed at the same time, for if they aren't, the leader will appear to be contradicting himself and the organization will be working against itself. For example, the leader cannot convert the organization to school-based decision making, while requiring a standard curriculum and instructional approach.

10. The restructuring leader would take the blame himself. The reason is that he wishes to encourage risk-taking and demonstrate his trust of subordinates. If there is a witch hunt every time problems develop, there is likely to be little entrepreneurship in the organization. Rather, subordinates will tend to stay with the tried and true. This will not develop the high levels of commitment, creativity, and persistence required to dramatically improve student achievement.

Some of my principals are ready for me to become a restructuring leader; others are not. The ones who aren't ready are doing a pretty good job. Do I wait until all are ready? Or do I interact differently with different principals? Or do I wait for some retirements?

You need to start exercising leadership for restructuring. All principals need to know that restructured schools are the preferred model. All principals should be expected to implement the elements of restructuring. You will need to take a developmental approach with those who are less ready. You may have to permit some who are very effective and who have the support of their teachers and parents to continue to operate as they have. You will want to take opportunities, however, to keep nudging them toward restructuring. Remember the manager who was fired even though his plant was exceeding company expectations for production. The manager was violating principles of the company and senior management was concerned that other managers, observing the success of the manager in question, would begin to model their practice after his.

You seem to be saying that policy and procedures don't matter any more—that we should abandon them and just let everyone make their own decisions. That doesn't make any sense to me. Could you clarify?

No, I don't mean to be saying that. Actually, policy will be necessary to implement restructuring. The kind of policy will just be different. For example, rather than have a uniform dress code, the policy might say that each school will insure that student attire does not interfere with academic work. This type of policy is liberating, rather than constricting. It allows for individual school variation. It permits an integration of concerns about student attire with curriclulum matters and the larger goals of the school.

I don't understand the need for a shift from the legal basis of authority to moral authority. I mean, I have to do what the law requires, don't I? Why wouldn't I cite the legal reason for taking the district in a certain direction or requesting certain activities of principals and teachers? I don't even know what moral authority is!

Moral authority is making decisions and taking action on the basis of what is good, just, and right. In many instances this may well also be what policy or the law requires. On occasion that might not be true, and you may have to operate under the old bureaucratic adage, "It is better to ask for forgiveness than permission." Even when your actions are sanctioned by law, you should justify them on a moral basis such as, "This is in the best interests of educating children for the 21st century," not on a legal basis.

The shift to moral authority is fundamental to restructuring, for it shifts the reason for action from compliance to commitment. To illustrate, you can *comply* with the law requiring you to have a discipline management plan, but you can become committed to helping each student develop himself fully as a person. You cannot become *committed* to developing a discipline management plan nor can you *comply* with a requirement that each student develop to his fullest (this "requirement" would be too vague to permit compliance). In addition to commitment, moral authority also compels attention to results whereas legal authority merely requires observation of the letter of the law or policy. A further reason for the shift to moral authority is that it is the only basis of authority that celebrates the autonomy of the individual; legal authority requires the conformity of the individual. Autonomy implies trust; conformity does not require trust, but rather evidence and monitoring. Thus a covenant is established between the leader and the subordinate, "I lead by moral authority and you accept the responsibility of the autonomy you are extended on the basis of moral authority by committing to achieve the full development of students who come under your care."

Implementation Checklist

_____ 1. I am practicing pull leadership.

_____ 2. Power is available in the organization and subordinates can attain it by becoming committed to a goal, attracting a team, and pressing for resources.

_____ 3. I utilize transformational leadership.

_____ 4. I base all organizational decisions on what is best for students, that is, what will help all students learn.

_____ 5. All of the members of the organization have a shared vision that is easily captured in a phrase or slogan.

_____ 6. All decisions in the organization are characterized by justice, fairness, and integrity.

_____ 7. Most decisions in the organization are made by consensus.

_____ 8. We have in place an accountability system, not a monitoring and compliance system.

_____ 9. There exists a clear expectation that all members of the organization will strive for the highest quality of service.

_____ 10. All members of the organization are expected to constantly seek to learn, and to guide their improvement efforts on the basis of research.

_____ 11. All members of the organization know the stages of change and accept that change cannot be seamless.

_____ 12. The board and school leaders are committed to holistic, rather than piecemeal, change.

_____ 13. There exists a commitment to collaborative leadership with a broad group of organizational members, not merely a few insiders.

_____ 14. A deep sense of the moral purpose of the work of the organization has been developed.

_____ 15. Leadership is seen as widespread in the organization. It is not limited to those who hold formal leadership titles.

_____ 16. Feedback to promote growth is given directly, caringly, and behaviorally.

_____ 17. Members of the organization know that the leadership has clout and uses it to shield them from undue pressures.

_____ 18. A high level of trust exists in the organization. Leaders and their subordinates know they can depend on each other.

_____ 19. Information is shared throughout the organization, the bad as well as the good.

_____ 20. Conflict is viewed as a sign of health. Processes exist by which conflict may be aired and resolved.

_____ 21. The culture of the organization has been altered to foster goal attainment.

_____ 22. There is congruity between ideals promoted and the decisions, policies, and budgets enacted.

_____ 23. Instructional leadership is a prime expectation of all organizational leaders.

References

1. Goldhammer, K. 1977. "Roles of the American School Superintendent, 1954-1974," in *Educational Administration: The Developing Decades*,

L. Cunningham, W. Hack, and R. Nystrand, eds., Berkeley, CA: Mc-Cutchen Publishing Corp.

2. Hoyle, J., F. English, and B. Steffy. 1985. *Skills for Successful School Leaders*. Arlington, VA: Association of School Administrators.

3. National Association of Secondary School Principals. 1985. *Performance-Based Preparation of Principals*. Reston, VA: The Association.

4. Batten, J. 1989. *Tough-Minded Leadership*. New York: AMACOM.

5. Bennis, W. and B. Nanus. 1985. *Leaders: Their Strategies for Taking Charge*. New York: Harper and Row.

6. Sergiovanni, T. Speech at the *Organization for Excellence Conference, Barton Creek Conference Center, Austin, TX, January 20, 1990*.

7. Kanter, R. 1983. *The Change Masters*. New York: Simon and Schuster, Inc.

8. Burns, J. 1978. *Leadership*. New York: Harper and Row.

9. Sergiovanni, T. and R. Starratt. 1988. *Supervision: Human Perspectives, 4th edition*. New York: McGraw-Hill.

10. Sergiovanni, T. 1990. *Value-Added Leadership*. New York: Harcourt Brace Jovanovich, Publishers.

11. Burns, J. loc. cit.

12. O Toole, J. 1985. *Vanguard Management*. Garden City, NY: Doubleday.

13. Sergiovanni, T. loc. cit.

14. Reavis, C. 1986. "How a Lighthouse Principal Revitalized His School," *NASSP Bulletin*, 70(492):44-439.

15. Peters, T. and N. Austin. 1985. *A Passion for Excellence*. New York: Random House.

16. Bennis, W. 1989. *On Becoming a Leader*. Reading, MA: Addison-Wesley.

17. Reavis, C. 1988. *Extraordinary Educators; Lessons in Leadership*. Bloomington, IN: Phi Delta Kappa.

18. Saxl, E., M. Miles, and A. Lieberman. 1989. *Assisting Change in Education*. Alexandria, VA: Association for Supervision and Curriculum Development.

19. Lead Restructuring Study Group Select Seminar, unpublished monograph, Xerox Training Center, Leesburg, VA (September 30-October 2, 1989).

20. Burns, J. loc. cit.

21. Bradford, D. and A Cohen. 1984. *Managing for Excellence*. New York: John Wiley and Sons.

22. Yukl, Gary. 1989. *Leadership in Organizations, 2nd edition*. Englewood Cliffs, NJ: Prentice Hall.

③ Skills Needed to Lead School Restructuring

To me the worst thing seems to be for a school principally to work with the methods of fear, force, and artificial authority.

ALBERT EINSTEIN [1]

To initiate a restructuring of school policies, programs, and practices a school system should first consider the skills and knowledge that personnel must possess, as there will be considerable variation in accordance with their individual experiences, aptitude, and awareness. Because restructuring constitutes both a macro change of the school district, school campus, and classroom, and a micro change of the practices and habits of all personnel, it is necessary to understand a host of operational techniques and skills. By skills we mean the "acquired ability to apply a given technique effectively and readily" [2].

The effectiveness of the restructured program will be partially dependent on how the school district answers the following questions in several key skill areas:

(1) How can *values* be used as *skill enablers* for school improvement among personnel from all parts of the organization?
(2) What specific *consensus* skills are needed for small groups to succeed whether in a faculty meeting, a vertical team problem-solving project, or a school board meeting?
(3) What are the dynamics of *small group* operations, and why is this an important skill?
(4) What are the techniques for building *teams* and what is the role of the *shared responsibility team*?

Values as Skill Enablers

In this chapter we will use the term *value* or *belief* to mean "what should be" [3]. As Bock has described, people in every society hold certain values about themselves, their families, community, and culture. These values are not random; they are integrated into a complex whole that makes sense to them even if they are unresolved and often contradictory. For example, we hold that every government should be representative of its people, but does that mean a representative should "mirror" his constituents, the activities of special interest groups, or that he should be free to act on his own individual values? The answers to these questions are conditioned by the context of the culture, community, and historical time period during which the question is asked.

In discussing values, three fundamental areas must be considered if they are to be skillfully used in a productive restructured school: (1) identification and definition of purpose, (2) understanding key criteria for setting organizational values, and (3) a description of the types of values that can be translated at all levels of the school organization.

These three areas contribute to an understanding of the larger role that values play in an organization. To make maximum use of values as skill enablers, each area must be considered as part of a whole.

Values as Integrators

There are essentially two factors critical to the purpose of values in an organization: they integrate actions within the organization, and they provide moral justification for decisions and actions. The first factor has to do with the general condition that we find in hundreds of school districts across the United States of America. A common trait among tens of thousands of school personnel, including teachers and administrators, is the general feeling of alienation and separation from the mission of the school organization. "We don't seem to be willing to take a stand for what is right" can be heard in the halls of thousands of schools.

This is a legitimate complaint about schools. Do all administrators, teachers, and custodians know what their school system is ready to stand for—to really fight for, to accomplish—or are most of the school personnel carrying out their specific responsibilities without reference to a common direction or as some say a vision? Put another way, what is the fiber that holds the organization together? Is it the traditional authority of the school organization or the classic power struggle between labor and management? As with a slightly used car, you can have the engine, the drive train, and even the ornaments of the latest educational innovations and fads, but what is the steering mechanism for your car and does it have a directional signal that benefits everyone involved?

Katz and Kahn [4] explain that organizations are a set of human "patterned interdependent activities" that are characterized by roles, norms, and values. Whereas roles, or what people do, are used to differentiate one job from another, values are used to integrate the organization. The importance of integration through values, though frequently ignored, cannot be overstated. Peters and Waterman [5] explain that "most businessmen are loath to write about, talk about, even take seriously value systems." Yet in virtually every case, the really successful organizations are "value-driven." The excellent organizations know what their core values are, and thus they know how to get where they are going. Schools are no different. We are all too ready to review budgets, debate reading programs, or formulate schedules. We let the essentials of day-to-day practice drive our actions, but where is the school district, school, and classroom going? Values provided the interlocking of parts of the total organization for a common purpose and direction. Values are important because they integrate and pull together the ideas and actions of individuals from all levels of the organization.

The process of integrating or weaving together the actions of the organization is largely dependent on the ability of the organization to provide a clear mental picture of where the organization is going. While some may call this "visioning" and others call it "goal-setting," it is essentially the process of constructing a common cognitive map for action that combines and galvanizes the efforts of all personnel.

Values Guide the Right Actions

Why do we need to identify a core set of values, when most school districts already have a goal-setting process for their schools? This is a good question when you consider that this is exactly how most school organizations operate. After all, goals provide direction, and the annual setting of long- and short-range goals should be sufficient to provide direction for the improvement of schools. However, the typical goal-setting process can be misleading if not even fatal to school personnel if there is no mental picture or cognitive map to guide the selection of the right actions.

James Thompson [6] points out that the process of defining goals is founded upon a desire to arrive at an intended "future domain." In his view, this process involves a group of highly interdependent individuals who "collectively have sufficient control of organizational resources to commit them in certain directions." From a functional viewpoint, it is true that traditional policy direction comes from the process of setting goals, but the major flaw of this approach is that the organization is subject to drift or serious miscalculation if a clear view of the values that underpin those goals is not maintained. For example, in a typical goal-setting process, many school districts are concerned about the issue of equity. Their stated goal is to "provide a quality education for every child." In one school district equity is interpreted to mean the regimented delivery of the curriculum for every child according to age, while in another district it means the de-standardization of the delivery of curriculum through a performance-based flexible continuous progress program. The differences between these two interpretations of equity are enormous, and understanding the underlying values associated with each approach has tremendous implications for goal-setting as well as for practices of many kinds in each district.

As we can see, the identification of goals, the coordination of activities, the supervision of staff, the interpretation of student results, and a myriad of other school activities are frequently ineffective without a clear and well-grounded understanding of the core organizational and educational values of the school. Values furnish the mental pictures or cognitive maps that influence people, and this facilitates the work and the many adjustments to changes that constantly occur in the dynamic school organization.

Values as a Moral Yardstick

Values do more than just integrate or weave together the parts of the organization. They also act as a moral or sacred yardstick – allowing a qualitative judgement about activities and decisions taken by those within the organization. This is the second factor in defining the purpose of values in the school organization. Simply put, values provide reason and justification for what is right in making thousands of decisions related to teaching and learning, as well as the actions of school boards, principals, central office staff and others.

According to Katz and Kahn [7] values become the beacon or "moral and social justification for actions within the organization." This is true for every aspect of action, whether it be a classroom set of rules for discipline or the district stance taken on policies for retention and social promotion. A clear example of values in action in schools is the way dropouts are treated by the school organization. Are dropouts treated with alternative recovery programs, special counseling, or additional programming? Or are they viewed as misfits within the traditional school organization, and not encouraged to come back? Any of the differences in action in the organization are based on the interpretation of what "should be" in the organization. Thus, values operate as a set of standards for judging a task or a behavior in the school organization.

Value-Driven Action

School teachers and others will support a group decision, even if their private opinions are not exactly similar, provided the group decision involves teachers and is made within the boundaries of values held by the organization. In the dynamic school organizations of the 1990s a commonly shared and articulated set of values or "should be's" gives legitimacy and coordination to hundreds of decisions that are made at all levels of the organization.

Criterion for Values

Values can be used as skill enablers within the restructured organization, provided that two criteria are met and well understood. The first criterion states that values must be beliefs that are appropriate for each individual *as a group member*. This criterion refers to the boundaries required in establishing a set of beliefs or values that indeed are perceived as worthy and that belong to all members of the school organization. Frequently, these values manifest themselves in rules for salary systems, hiring practices, work hours and work loads, guidelines for discipline, student promotion, grading, and a host of other regulations. The school system might pay careful attention to being consistent and "appropriate" with role-alike members—teacher to teacher, custodian to custodian—however, violations of this criterion frequently occur when differential treatment occurs between groups.

Take the area of training, for instance. In many of America's school systems it is the school board and central office staff who participate in conferences and training programs, while the average classroom teacher is removed from the mainstream of contemporary school improvement efforts with little or no chance to visit other school sites or to grow from other professional activities. If training and professional growth is valued by all members, but only one group participates, then conflict will grow geometrically with the number of members denied the same opportunity. This condition has become prevalent in the schools of the 1980s and will only become increasingly problematic for the schools of the 1990s.

The second criterion for defining the values of the organization is that there should be a *general commonality* for the belief with high *group awareness of acceptance*. As Katz and Kahn [8] further point out, organizations can self-destruct with anarchy if each individual is allowed to operate totally by his own rules or guidelines. Because organizations exist as patterned sets of relationships, recognizing and then accepting a common set of core values is essential to group cohesion and success. The recognition of core values comes from articulation through discussion, debate and conflict. Conflict over the values that any group holds is particularly healthy to the reconstructed organization, as it clarifies what "should be" and solidifies the members of the group into a purposeful organization. Without conflict – conflict that illuminates what is valued among the members of the organization – each individual is bound to follow his or her own separate way, to remain segmented and fragmented as an isolated, unconnected part of a larger organization. It does not matter that a number of individual members of the group may possess differing or even conflicting views of the core articulated values, as long as a large majority is in agreement.

Thus, these two criteria for defining core values are essential to nurturing the success of the restructured school. Individuals as members of a group – whether at the departmental, school, or district level – must adhere to a core set of values that are both appropriate to the group and have high awareness for group acceptance of those values. There are essentially two types of organizational values that are in operation within organizations: *sacred* (or moral) and *pragmatic* values.

Sacred Values

Public schools have a higher purpose than most organizations. Their purpose can be viewed as both unique and sacred when compared to other governmental agencies and private sector businesses. In the history of public schooling, beginning with the first compulsory attendance law in 1852 in Massachusetts, public education has existed to help families socialize their children in an increasingly complex industrial world, to extend the principles of democracy and advance our collective sense of manifest destiny, and finally, to "provide equal opportunity and maintain fair access to social status and reward" [9]. These three evolving themes have dominated the American educational landscape over the past 150 years, and they sustain a sense of larger purpose for the teachers that serve this profession.

The moral values that are viewed as sacred and unique to the professionals of a school system can vary with each community and school setting, but generally these examples fit the restructured school organization of the future.

- *We believe that all children can learn.* This value has many practical and operational implications, but it maintains a significant moral dimension for the future of our schools that is critical to the success of all school-age children.
- *We believe that every person is to be treated with dignity and respect.* It seems obvious that this should be a commonly held sacred value, but schools often falter here, particularly when some parents or children treat school teachers with rude and unacceptable behavior, while our schools and school professionals also can be very disinviting to many parents and children.
- *Each child will be held responsible for his or her own behavior.* This is often a commonly held value that is regularly practiced in a contradictory way, as most professionals in schools will assume the role of responsibility for student behavior with homework, grading, and other control practices common to many schools.

The above examples of core or sacred values are not easily attained in most school districts. They frequently go unstated or can even run counter to the moral practices of school personnel, in which case this becomes a violation of the first criterion. Many states have been making a series of top-down decisions to standardize the movement of children through a grade level testing and curriculum program. These efforts to standardize have been met with stiff teacher opposition, as they run counter to the value of treating children individually, or they were simply not commonly accepted or acknowledged by enough members of the schools—thus violating the second criterion. There are other sacred values that schools do share with other businesses, industries, and governmental agencies. Organizations of many types have a strong belief in positive work attitudes, loyalty, and cleanliness. These values often permeate the entire organization without discussion or debate, yet they remain powerful tools for uniting employee behavior. These values are not always obvious within the school organization. Here are a few examples of how to state these as core or moral values:

- Children must not feel unwanted by school personnel.
- We must not allow any teacher to feel that he/she is less important than another.
- We must not tear down others when we can build them up.
- We will act and dress like professionals.

Pragmatic Values

Every organization is permeated by a set of pragmatic values. They are neither sacred nor moral in character, but they are vital "should be's" to the overall operation of the organization. In the restructured school there are a set of pragmatic values that are essential to the success of professionals and children alike in the 1990s and beyond. Stated as core pragmatic beliefs, here are a few critical examples:

- We will create participatory work settings that prize involvement and opportunities for influence.
- We will establish clear, attainable, and professional expectations and goals and assist staff in attaining them.
- We will support our staff with appropriate training, continuous feedback, and a non-threatening environment in which to work.
- We will strive to work openly and continuously with our school community to promote understanding and support of our work as professionals.
- We will base our decisions on data and the best information available.

These pragmatic values are critical to the success of the restructured school organization, but they cannot necessarily be considered sacred core values. School organizations need to become more open and flexible with their environment, thus they are able to change with time and become more relevant to the cultural values of the 1990s and beyond to the 21st century.

It is pointed out by Katz and Kahn [10] that individuals with common values "find it intrinsically rewarding to work for the fulfillment of their beliefs," a fact that is demonstrated by the success of many volunteer organizations. The feeling of coming together as a school community is not likely to arise unless individuals have a shared set of values, a true understanding and respect for varying opinions, and a willingness to speak and act in a manner that is consistent with making honest and straightforward decisions.

Consensus as a Skill Enabler

The great unifying theme at the conclusion of the 20th century is the triumph of the individual. Threatened by totalitarianism for much of this century, individuals are meeting the millennium more powerful than ever before. . . . Yet it does not mean the individual is condemned to face the world alone. Stripped down to the individual, one can build community, the free association of individuals. In community there is no place to hide either. Everyone knows who is contributing, who is not.

NAISBITT, 1990 [11]

The schools of the 1990s and beyond are going to be increasingly skeptical of autocratic methods or mass movement actions such as those we have seen in the last fifty years of American education. Teachers and other professionals want to work in school settings that allow individualism to flourish in a nurturing, cooperative, and collegial environment. The teaching professionals of America are looking for a sense of cohesion among their respective colleagues and parents. This can happen in the restructured environment when school professionals have access to skills that allow them as individuals to have a meaningful role in group settings.

School professionals often find themselves working in small group settings, and at any one time each individual is in a position to influence a decision, but the quality of this influence is largely affected by the ability of these individuals to arrive at a collective agreement and acceptance of their ideas and suggestions. Oftentimes you can find individuals who have a natural talent or unique intuition for gaining group support and understanding, but anyone can acquire this skill provided they are given the right tools for doing so. Consensus is such a tool. It is an enabling skill that can help anyone become more effective and more productive in the overall operation of a high-performing group within a school.

The present day notion of consensus as a skill enabler for the restructured school organizations is rooted in the original Latin meaning of "consensus." In the late twentieth century the term *consensus* has come to mean "agreement, especially in opinion" [12], but centuries ago the Latin term *sentiere* meant "to feel" with the prefix *con* meaning "with" or "together." According to Pfeffer, consensus "facilitates cohesion and a common position within the subunit" [13]. Thus, consensus really means to come together or to feel together as a community within a group.

There are four key conditions that must be considered to generate consensus—that is, to generate a feeling of community among individuals within a group.

(1) The assignment of purposeful and rewarding roles for each group throughout the district.
(2) The promotion of district and school objectives through face-to-face encounters where colleagues experience the satisfaction of helping, supporting, and reinforcing each other.

(3) The use of participatory management techniques where professionals see on their own, create something from their own effort, and act on critical decisions that have major impact on the school.
(4) The sharing of rewards from common work and effort.

These conditions form the basis for working together in a consensus-based environment. We will examine each individually.

Purposeful and Rewarding Roles

Activating a group that has a real mission and function that goes beyond the daily maintenance of school operations is highly satisfying to teachers and other professionals. This is at the heart of what *empowerment* means in the restructured school. Ernest Boyer, President of the Carnegie Foundation for the Advancement of Teaching, states that empowerment means to engage teachers in "the education mission, excite them about the goals, and involve them in deciding what to teach, what materials to use, and how to assess students" [14]. This is a condition that can easily be overlooked. Here are a few examples.

- election to a district-wide communications committee designed to act as a conduit of information that can result in a number of significant actions within a school or school district
- appointment or election to a districtwide Instructional Leadership Council; this group would be responsible for screening and initiating decisions about the educational philosophy, programs, and practices
- formation of a salary and benefits council that would meet on a regular basis to review and make recommendations to the school board; it would be best to include business leaders and parents, so that the efforts of this group do not seem to be self-serving
- formation of campus leadership teams that would function as decision-making groups and clearinghouses for continued improvement; these groups could easily link with any districtwide group

The next condition refers to the importance of having opportunities for good interpersonal relations among all group members.

Face-to-Face Encounters

This condition is akin to the notion of managing by walking around, as described by Peters and others. Too often the "grand tour" through a school is not enough to understand or share the needs and desires of classroom teachers. In hundreds of school systems across America, the visit to a school is limited to only the cafeteria or principals' offices. Principals and superintendents must be willing to stop, look, and listen in both informal and formal settings face-to-face with teachers. No memo or speech can compensate for the value of eyeball-to-eyeball discussion, and it must be continuous throughout the year.

Participatory Management Techniques

There is a high degree of readiness for quality participation in the teaching profession. Ann Lewis [15] reports in a American Association of School Administrators survey that administrators and teachers have similar views about the potential for seeing and acting on their own to make decisions of importance. When asked what each group thought of recent management trends in education, they responded as shown in Table 1 (in percents).

As you can see there is a high degree of readiness for altering the conditions of operation in schools. Teachers, even more than administrators, are ready to assume greater responsibility for working together to solve their own classroom teaching and learning problems. They are ready to assume the responsibility for improving policies and procedures when they have a part in seeing that this process is of their own doing. In a summary of the recent research on teacher participation, Duttweiler [16] points out that teacher satisfaction will increase with the greater challenge of participation, but

TABLE 1

		Administrators		Teachers	
		yes	no	yes	no
1.	Providing more individualized instruction to teachers	70.0	16.2	77.9	20.8
2.	Reorganizing faculty practices (e.g., differentiated staffing/flexible scheduling)	50.7	39.6	53.7	40.0
3.	Establishing restructured experiments	36.2	52.6	68.7	25.0
4.	Restructuring of teaching methods (e.g., cooperative learining)	58.2	30.6	78.1	18.7
5.	Restructuring of curriculum	49.2	41.8	56.2	36.2
6.	Giving greater authority to the school	61.8	30.9	75.6	19.4
7.	Giving greater authority to teachers	41.9	49.2	42.2	45.3
8.	Providing more support for teachers (e.g., increased salaries, reduced teaching loads)	43.4	47.7	87.5	9.4

All figures are rounded off, and the "No response" answers are not reported here.

student outcomes will also improve. The research on effective principals further corroborates this conclusion, as studies show that improved delegation techniques lead to improved decisions that are more timely and efficient.

The Sharing of Rewards

The fourth condition, which is so essential to the integration of effort and to creating a sense of community among teachers and principals, is more difficult to achieve in the public school setting. One of the most inhibiting problems in schools, and one which is not present in private sector businesses and industries, is the absence of a good promotion system for highly effective teachers. Teachers work in community environments that make it very difficult to single out exemplary individual performance, as evidenced by the meager results that merit pay and career ladder systems have shown in numerous states in the 1980s. Regardless, there is a promising trend in practice toward giving whole school rewards for outstanding performance. It is not improbable to assume that campus-based decisions should be rewarded with campus-level rewards, such as new equipment and additional staff. Duttweiler [17] suggests that reduced job stress is a meaningful benefit of participation for individual employees, but in a study from Newark, New Jersey, teachers ranked the following two items as the highest rewards and incentives that can be given to teachers:

- having input into policy-making and participating in educational decision making
- participating in curriculum development, working with other teachers, and developing and presenting workshops

Techniques for Achieving Consensus

What are the specific skills that school professionals and others can use to work to achieve consensus, particularly in a complex arena like teaching and learning? There are a number of techniques that make consensus an effective enabling tool—brainstorming and clarification, for example, are two fundamental skills. In a more structured vein, the Delphi and Nominal Group Techniques are both proven methods for working in a cooperative school environment. Before we describe these powerful techniques, it is essential to point out that none of them involve the use of voting. Voting is debilitating and counterproductive to a faculty or a group of professionals working to solve their own problems. With voting there are winners and losers, and it is very difficult for any group to arrive at a feeling of community when every time a decision is made it only requires agreement by 51% of the participants. In the consensus-based setting, everyone is compelled to resolve their own differences *before* a decision is actually made.

Brainstorming and Clarification

Brainstorming and clarification can be used very effectively in group settings. In brainstorming, group members are simply asked to list their ideas about a problem or situation. Their ideas, whether good or not, are all accepted without subjective comment by anyone in the group. It is assumed that not all ideas will necessarily be useful or appropriate to the group, so the members are encouraged to be as creative as possible.

Clarification is employed after the listing of ideas, but the clarification of a particular idea should not always come from the person who originally mentioned that idea. The group should try to have a second person do the clarifying and should be sure that different members take turns clarifying each other's comments. This will be difficult to do at first—in fact, it may be necessary to return to the person who originated the idea a few times for clarification—but after a few tries the group will come to discover that no one person has to have individual ownership over any one idea.

Once an idea is listed and efforts have been made to clarify it, then the whole group has an opportunity to own the idea. Following this step, the ideas can then be evaluated for their quality, the untenable ones can be immediately discarded, and the group can arrive at agreement over the best ideas to pursue. It may be necessary to use a "bridging" concept to link together two similar but competing ideas, or an "umbrella" concept to pull two ideas together at a higher level. It may even be necessary to redefine terminology, as this is frequently the cause of blocks experienced by groups seeking consensus. Remember, in achieving consensus it is essential that no votes be taken, in order to maintain the commitment from everyone.

One of the advantages of this simple but effective process is that everyone can have equal status in the group. It may be necessary to appoint a group reporter and recorder (they should be separate people), but the value of authority and position are minimized particularly if it is a vertical group setting. Another advantage to this technique is the actual generation of ideas that can emerge from the group. In general, American schools have been reluctant to allow ideas to percolate to the top of the school organization. Toyota, one of the largest and most successful industrial companies in the world, uses a variety of techniques to generate ideas from throughout their company. As Kenichi Ohmae [18] points out,

> Back in the 1950s, the company's 45,000 employees turned in only a few hundred suggestions to their suggestion box annually. Today, still employing 45,000 Toyota gets 900,000 proposals—20 per employee in the average—per year, worth $230 million a year in savings.

This is in remarkable contrast with how schools operate. Brainstorming and clarification are two fundamental tools that can enable groups to work together smoothly and efficiently.

It is important to keep in mind that no matter what process or model you use, conflict is not to be avoided and it is expected that everyone will not agree with all aspects of any decision. Consensus is designed to acquire the best solutions with the greatest degree of acceptance by everyone involved or affected.

The Delphi and Nominal Group Techniques (NGT) are two of the most advanced and proven methods for helping groups of all sizes and types to arrive at widespread agreement on solutions to problems. They are similar in that they both emphasize pooling ideas from individuals working independently of each other [19]. In the Delphi process individuals typically complete a questionnaire, while in the NGT process participants record their responses in silence but in the presence of each other. In both techniques, the responses are pooled together. The Delphi respondents turn in their questionnaires for pooling, and the NGT respondents use a round-robin process to write their answers on tear sheets or chalkboards. The responses are then evaluated, and mathematical voting (rank ordering or rating) is used to arrive at an aggregate decision. The major difference between these techniques is that the Delphi is completed through the mail, while the NTG is completed face-to-face throughout the procedure. A significant advantage to both techniques is the "equality of participation" [20] experienced by each member of the group.

Nominal Group Technique (NGT)

The NGT system as described by Delbecq can be used with a high degree of effectiveness if careful attention is given to preparing and outlining the group process in advance. Since the participants are going to be using paper and pencil, they will need adequate writing areas, preferably at a table that is rectangular with one end open for flip chart use.

It is essential to pay careful attention to having the right supplies:

- flip chart at each table

- rolls of masking tape
- packs of 3×5 cards for each table
- flip chart pens for each table
- paper and pencil for everyone

The flip chart is important because ideas will be revealed to everyone once the initial writing is completed. There are five essential steps to completing the NGT process.

Step 1: Silent Generation of Ideas

To begin, a NGT question in written form is addressed to each group. Then the question is read, and the members of the group are asked to write ideas or phrases in brief form silently. The questions can vary from "What should be our instructional goals for this year?" to "How can consensus technique be effective in your school?" Clarifications are to be resisted, and silence is essential.

Step 2: Round-Robin Recording of Ideas

Members of the group are asked to contribute one idea or phrase in round-robin fashion. Then each idea is put on the flip chart. This encourages participation and increases a tolerance of ideas from everyone. It is important to record quickly and in the words of the participants. The organizer should keep going around tearing the flip chart sheets off to put on the wall until all ideas are expressed.

Step 3: Serial Discussion for Clarification

Here each idea is discussed in order, with opportunity for individual clarification. It is important to flush out the meaning of an idea, allowing varying opinion to emerge, but the pace should be fairly rapid to keep things moving. It is important *not to allow* members of the group to clarify their own ideas, as this could inhibit discussion when "bosses" or other influential people are in the group.

Step 4: Preliminary Vote on Item Importance

The serial discussion has enhanced the understanding of each item. The logic and pros and cons were more easily understood, but now individual judgements must be aggregated to arrive at a group decision. First, individual members should rank order the items, and then the mean is used to arrive at a group discussion. The items are discussed again, and then a revote is taken to arrive at a final conclusion. Here is a recommended method for pooling agreement:

(1) Have the group select a specific number of most important items—usually five is a good number.
   - Using 3×5 cards each member selects one item for each card. This should be done individually.
   - Now each member should rank order their cards one at a time.
(2) Now the cards are collected and, after shuffling them, the ranking is recorded in front of everyone. Do not vote, as the ranking will help push consensus.

Normally, it is not necessary to go beyond this step, but it is often necessary to redo the pooling of ranked responses if consensus is not very clear.

Step 5: Final Ranking

It may not be necessary to use this step, but it is possible to further refine the ranking by putting each of the top five to seven items on a ten-point scale, with one being least and ten most important. As Delbecq [21] points out, the NGT is useful as a group decision process to identify elements of a problem situation and to establish priorities where individual opinions must be aggregated into a group decision.

Delphi Technique

The Delphi Technique (DT), Delbecq argues, can be used to arrive at a group agreement, but it was first used to pool expert opinion of individuals who could not attend a group meeting. The DT is essentially a series of questionnaires that get passed through the mail in a continually refined step method. It is especially helpful for pre-planning a workshop, because in this way it is possible to gauge the opinions of participants about seminar material that they may not be familiar with yet. It does take time to develop the questions, but significant meeting time can be saved in the process. It is important to distribute the results of the questionnaire survey to all participants so they can see the average responses in degree of importance.

Three Consensus Models

The techniques of brainstorming, clarification, Nominal Group, and Delta Technique are extremely useful in helping groups to achieve their objectives. These techniques can be useful in both planning and problem-solving situations. In summary, we have adopted an outline from James Lewis [22] where he describes the two consensus models that are most commonly used in work settings. Each consensus model is highly adaptable to the extensive use of brainstorming, clarification, and the Delphi and Nominal Group Techniques.

Group Consensus Model

This model uses a series of groups that all flow like a pyramid to the top of the organization. The origination of ideas begins with the bottom-level groups, and the number of ideas are increasingly reduced or screened by subsequent groups up the chain-of-command of the company.

There are four steps for implementation.

(1) The first group uses idea generation through brainstorming, and this can involve as many as a hundred or more participants.
(2) The next group, which can consist of as many as ten to fifteen participants, then screens down to the ten to twenty best ideas.
(3) This third group then selects the best five ideas for action.
(4) Finally, the last group will whittle down to the two best ideas, and use consensus to arrive at the best decision. The number of ideas will vary with how many groups there are to begin with.

The pyramid is used with the supervisors getting involved only in the later stages, after the ideas have already been generated.

Quaker Consensus Model

This model establishes a list of behaviors that each participant must follow, thus serving as a "code of conduct" in the process. The rules state

- Do not argue your own point of view or opinion.
- Have everyone be a winner.
- Do not change your mind to avoid conflict or differences.
- View differences as good and useful.
- Do not vote under any circumstances.
- Be skeptical about early agreement.

The use of this technique is different in that there is no prescribed method of operation, since there is a code of conduct that is used to guide the behavior of the group. An important factor can be added by stating that anyone can block a group decision. Everyone has to be in agreement, thus the group will have to keep working at solving the problem or making the decision until there is complete agreement.

Small Group Dynamics as a Skill Enabler

It has become a cliche that to restore our global competitiveness, we need to reform our educational system. This will take a lot more than money.

HENRY GRUNWALD [23]

What are the dynamics of small group operations, and why is knowledge of this an important enabling skill for achieving the shared responsibility team? The school leaders of the 1990s are faced with a daunting array of financial, personnel, organizational, and student learning problems. These problems can seem overwhelming to educational leaders, particularly when individuals working in groups around the leaders are unfamiliar with the stages of group dynamics that are so well documented in the field of management science.

Leaders often feel that they have to be the problem solvers, taking responsibility for quality control, seeing to it that other personnel are motivated, and shouldering a host of other leadership burdens. The irony of this condition is that essentially it is the groups themselves and not the leaders that can best assume the responsibility for producing optimum solutions and results. Bradford and Cohen[24] elaborate on the importance of building *shared responsibility teams* for improved organizational performance, but first it is critical to identify the dynamics of small group development.

Bradford and Cohen identify five stages of group development, which can be understood as being progressive and inextricably linked together. The five stages from simple to complex are: (1) membership, (2) subgrouping, (3) confrontation, (4) individual differentiation, and (5) shared responsibility. The goal of every group should be to reach the shared responsibility stage, but this is the most difficult to achieve as most groups have a hard time getting past earlier stages. Some groups will go to the confrontation stage, but sometimes they fall back to subgrouping when members are seeking to avoid confrontation or are frustrated with the results of the confrontation. When a group has moved past the confrontation stage its members often become satisfied with the differentiation stage, and rarely reach true organizational excellence. In describing the five stages it is possible to examine the stage that any group is at by looking at these six behavioral areas:

- atmosphere and relationships

- goal understanding and acceptance
- listening and information sharing
- decision making
- reaction to leadership
- attention to the way the group is working

Stage 1: Membership

It is easy to identify with the membership stage. This is the point at which a group such as a task force or standing committee will come together to meet for the first few times. Members are tentative with each other, unsure of their standing in the group with a boss or other persons not as familiar as others. Individuals feel isolated and they are constantly "sizing-up" the leader of the group. There is normally a feeling of frustration and extreme caution by most members. In examining the six behavioral areas it is easy to identify with these characteristics, as shown in Table 2.

These characteristics are common to most newly formed groups when they meet their first few times. As the group becomes more comfortable over time, it begins to enter the second stage of group development—the subgrouping stage.

Stage 2: Subgrouping

In this stage members of the group begin to look for other members they can identify with, and then they begin to divide into factions or subgroupings. Though many of the differences between subgroups are artificial and are more perceived than real, one can spot a lot of factional behavior and posturing as demonstrated by an "us against

TABLE 2

1.	Atmosphere and relations	Cautious, feelings suppressed, low conflict, few outbursts
2.	Goal understanding and acceptance	Low, fuzzy
3.	Listening and information sharing	Intense, but high distortion and low disclosure
4.	Decision making	Dominated by only the active members
5.	Reaction to leadership	Tested by members, tentative
6.	Attention to the way the group is working	Ignored

them" mentality. At this stage, members will reserve their true feelings and comments for members of their subgroup in the hallway at the break, or for the office later in the day where they feel comfortable to criticize other subgroups that have emerged. This is when the leader needs to be a little mouse in the hallway at the break so he can find out how people really think. The six behavioral characteristics of this stage are shown in Table 3.

At this stage, members are beginning to become familiar with a few chosen members of their group, and there is increased awareness of what the group is to accomplish, but leadership continues to fall almost entirely in the hands of the leader. Quite frankly, most leaders are very comfortable with this stage as they affirm their value and importance.

Stage 3: Confrontation

Most leaders are very reluctant to allow their group to go to the confrontational stage. After all, the carefully laid plans for achievement can fall apart with too much conflict. This is unfortunate because most jobs and products will suffer if members are hiding and disguising their real thoughts and feelings. One can imagine the implications of not allowing a group to enter the stage of confrontation when, for example, a team of engineers is redesigning a pressure valve in a chemical plant that powers products with highly flammable fuel. Is this any less important when the discussion or task is to improve the math program of 10,000 children in a school district? The characteristics of the confrontation stage are shown in Table 4.

Members reach the confrontation stage when they tire of withholding their true feelings and they begin to exhibit more aggressive behavior. Members of different subgroups are seeking to exert influence over the discussion and outcomes of the meeting. Arguments begin to surface between subgroupings, and individuals become entrenched in their early positions. The confrontation becomes frustrating to many individual members, but eventually the discussion begins to crystallize as differing and competing philosophies surface.

It is, in fact, very important that groups experience confrontation for clarification and understanding to emerge. Groups need to resolve their factional or individual differences, and frequently confrontation will have a beneficial effect on the ultimate outcome or decision. Once the group has experienced confrontation it can fall back to the prior stage of subgrouping or move into stage four, individual differentiation. Many groups reach the fourth stage and go on to successfully ac-

TABLE 3

1.	Atmosphere and relationships	Increasing closeness within subgroup, cross-group criticism, false unanimity
2.	Goal understanding and acceptance	Increasing clarity, misperseptions continue
3.	Listening and information sharing	Similarities within subgroups not as great as perceived
4.	Decision making	Fragmented, deadlocks, to the boss by default
5.	Reaction to leadership	Resisted, often covertly
6.	Attention to the way the group is working	Noticed but avoided, discussed outside meeting in small groups

You can assume that often this regression to stage two is highly correlated either with a lack of leadership or with the degree to which individuals are governed by persistent bureaucratic rules and procedures that they cannot break out of or influence.

Stage 4: Individual Differentiation

This stage is characterized by relief that, in fact, individuals can resolve difficult problems. Members of the group no longer cling only to their earlier subgroupings, as the members now circulate in new subgroupings with no unusual loyalty to any one group. The individual differentiation stage can be very productive, with individuals receiving new jobs to perform with little resistance from the group. The agenda moves quickly as jobs are parceled out and the expectation exists for individual resolution of the problems. The group's goals are well understood, a kinship exists among team mem-

TABLE 4

1.	Atmosphere and relationships	Hostility beteen subgroups
2.	Goal understanding and acceptance	Up for grabs, fought over
3.	Listening and infromation sharing	Poor
4.	Decision making	Dominated by the most powerful and loudest
5.	Reaction to leadership	Power struggles, jockeying for position
6.	Attention to the way the group is working	Used as a weapon against perceived opponents

bers, and multiple issues are brought up, though rarely in a problem-solving mode. The characteristics of this stage are shown in Table 5.

Stage four can be viewed as a productive level of operation for most groups. At this stage, the group is effective in giving jobs to members and in discussing any number of issues, and the comfort for taking on differing jobs by individuals is widely accepted. The problem with this level occurs when there is opportunity for intensive planning and problem solving. Stage four does not lend itself to true collaboration and high-energy commitment to a task to be completed. Everything is still segmented among members of the group, and the leader retains a controlling or directing (see Chapter 2) stance. At stage four, members of the group are pleased with segmenting and piecing out the work, but if the task requires a high degree of commitment to significantly alter existing practices, then only the shared responsibility team can successfully accomplish the task. The shared responsibility team defines much of the difference between a "well-operating" group and an "excellently operating" group.

Stage 5: Shared Responsibility

In stage five of the Bradford and Cohen [29] model, the organization makes the transformation from "group" to "team." This is the most "actualized" of all group stages. Individuals, regardless of position or power in the organization, are each valued for the expertise that they can bring to the group. At this stage of development, each person is keenly aware of his or her goals and group expectations, while control mechanisms are limited to the best information and the task at hand.

TABLE 5

1.	Atmosphere and relationships	Confident, satisfied, open honest differences
2.	Goal understanding and acceptance	Agreed on by most
3.	Listening and infromation sharing	Reasonably good
4.	Decision making	Based on individual expertise, often done by the boss in consultation with others
5.	Reaction to leadership	General support, individual differences in influence
6.	Attention to the way the group is working	Alternates between uncritical or overcompulsive discussion

each working to improve the product or decision they are charged with. Agenda items are filled with important issues—Bradford and Cohen [30] suggest that there should always be a 15% challenge—and the work of the group is persistently businesslike.

In a true stage five experience the group will have its own self-correcting mechanisms for staying the course of problem resolution. The success of the group will no longer depend entirely on the leader, as other members assume the leadership roles the situation calls for. Bradford and Cohen [31] describe the characteristics of the shared responsibility team in Table 6.

The development of the shared responsibility team for school operations represents the best of all working conditions that can be created for professional educators. The team becomes one that is characterized as democratic, flexible, and energized to act on its own for the benefit of the task it is to accomplish. This advanced stage of development suggests that careful attention should be given to an array of critical enabling skills.

Teaming as a Skill Enabler

The command-and-control model of management will be a relic of the past as the information-based organization becomes the norm.
AMERICAN RENAISSANCE [25]

The public schools of the 1990s are operating in a rapidly changing and ever-divergent environment. With the locus of authority varying between state and local leaders, public school leaders recognize the importance of having teams to disseminate information and to review

TABLE 6

1.	Atmosphere and relationships	Supportive, open , expressive varied, disagreement resolved promptly
2.	Goal understanding and acceptance	Committed to the larger goals of the district
3.	Listening and information sharing	Excellent, rapid, and direct
4.	Decision making	By consensus: Collective when all resources are needed, and individual when one expert is necessary (but not always the boss)
5.	Attention to the way the group is working	Discussed as needed, to support the task to be accomplished, and anyone can initiate the discussion, support, or solution

and take action on problems. In the increasingly complex and ambiguous environments in which public school educators find themselves, the teaming approach can be a highly satisfying and productive way to operate. There are significant differences between the traditional industrial model of operation that is found in most school districts and the teaming program. Hanson [26] describes the dichotomy that Rensis Likert recognized between four forms of design with the classical bureaucratic system (System 1) at one end and the teaming system (System 4) at the other end. This is illustrated in Table 7.

The teaming structure is significantly different from the traditional structure insofar as the treatment of individuals throughout the development of the skills of individuals at all levels of the organization. From the perspective of organizational design, Robey [27] describes how "lateral teams drawn from different departments in an organization" have become an integral part of the operations of construction companies, banks, chemical plants, and many other busi-

Table 7

System 1 (Classical Structure)	System 4 (Teaming Structure)
1. Leadership Operations	
No trust and confidence in those around you; no mutual support for problem solving	Complete trust and confidence in those working for you, which is reciprocated
2. Motivational Forces	
Tap physical and economic needs only through use of punishment and rewards; work attitudes are unfavorable	Tap full range of employee needs; favorable work attitudes by all employees
3. Communication	
Downward and from the top; limited in scope and met with suspicion; anything from the bottom met with inaccuracy and distortion	Flows feely in all direction; initiated at any level; tends to be complete
4. Interaction-Influence Process	
Limited, cooperation and teamwork is absent; employees have limited influence	Open, cooperative, and good teamwork, employees have large influence on goals, methods
5. Control	
Managed from the top and punitive in nature	Spread throughout, emphasis on self-control and self-guidance for problem solving
6. Training	
Limited training resources	Abundant at all levels

nesses. These lateral teams permeate all layers of the organization and are frequently charged with making major decisions for improvement. This pooling of expertise necessitates a high level of interdependence and adjustment by individuals from widely dispersed parts of the organization. Thus, under these conditions interdependent groups can maximize their performance in the shared responsibility mode.

Marvin Weisbord [28] affirms that the teaming concept will work when four conditions are met:

(1) Interdependence—The team has to be working on problems of importance that every individual has a vested interest in. The members of the team need to have a feeling that their success depends on their ability to work together.
(2) Leadership—The leader has to be willing to take the risks of participation.
(3) Joint Decision—This is where all members agree to participate.
(4) Equal Influence—Every member of the team has an opportunity to influence the items that are placed in the agenda.

The process of converting the traditional industrial model of school organization to one that elevates the role of each individual in a high-achievement, participatory environment argues for a careful review of the micro skills of everyone involved. Kenichi Ohmae [32] explains that contemporary systems often fail because of three limits that he calls his "essential R's"—reality, ripeness, and resources. The problem of reality refers to the difficulty of staying sensitive to the needs of consumers, the competition, and the company's field of competence, while ripeness refers to the difficulty of being timely when making strategic corporate changes.

A change in strategy by any organization is bound to fail if it is introduced prematurely or if it is introduced too late to take advantage of market shifts. The problem of being too slow to anticipate future market shifts has characterized much of the American business experience over the last twenty years. American public school systems are guilty of the same error of responsiveness and predictiveness. Significant changes through heightened expectations, an increasingly competitive world economy, and expanding student diversity have placed the public schools in the critical position of needing to restructure the design, practices, and habits of professional educators.

The third essential problem, that of resources, involves more than simply the problems of money. Ohme [33] points out that it is nothing short of astonishing that skills are so easily overlooked in business systems. The success rate of chemical companies taking on food processing or food companies moving into electronics is very low. Though the industrial landscape is littered with failed diversification efforts, the basic reason for much of this failure is the lack of "sensitivity to the limitations of their own internal resources and skills."

An important parallel can be drawn between the changes that American business systems have begun to slowly undertake in the past decade and the position that schools find themselves in for the 1990s. School and community leaders must pay careful attention to the skill demands that a high-achievement environment demands. As described in this chapter, values—both sacred and pragmatic—can be useful skill enablers for the work and improvement activities of all personnel. There is a widespread recognition that school personnel must improve efforts at vertical as well as horizontal integration, and a practiced set of consensus skills can enable groups at any level to become effective problem solvers and planners. In addition, understanding the dynamics of small group operations and the techniques for building groups into shared responsibility teams can empower all staff with the right combination of skills for a more successful and productive restructured school system.

Troubleshooting

I understand the importance of values, but I'm still not sure what to do first in order to establish these. I can envision a quick meeting in which all involved vote for apple pie, motherhood, and the flag, but make no real commitment to evolve. You seem to envision something more compelling. How do you keep the sessions of values from being superficial?

It is good that you recognize the importance of values. Many leaders tend to rush past this stage, feeling that all school people share essentially the same values. Yet, if values are not firmly established, no basis exists for the other skills discussed in this chapter. Now to your question. In the first meeting it is very important to set the right tone. The people at that meeting should be people of high visibility and high influence, and should be drawn from both the professional staff and the community.

You might want to say something like this—"In the past, from time to time, we have stated values in this district and then gone on largely to ignore them. Things are going to be different this time around. Once these values are established, we intend to base all of our decisions on them—budgets, personnel, curriculum and so forth. Consequently, it is very important that you consider very carefully the values you agree on." All values will be agreed on by consensus, because it is critical that all participants be able to fully support these values. It could take up to a year to reach a clear set of values that everyone agrees on and fully supports. Once you get them, however, they will provide a road map for your district for the next several years.

You must assure the team that you will back them in terms of full secretarial support and supplies, and you must make it clear that there is no more important task before your district at this time. As ideas are put forward, you may act as the devil's advocate. For example, if group members agree that all children can learn, you may question if they really mean that. Point out the implications. At the same time, you have to press them to articulate high goals. After all, those are the only ones that motivate people to high levels of commitment and achievement. By what you say, by what you do, and by stating a fairly lengthy time line, you will convey the importance you attach to the value statements.

Some of my people are pretty opinionated. I'm not sure they could ever get to the point of decision making by consensus.

One of the keys to this problem is to gain wide-ranging support throughout the district for the values that you and your leadership team develop. It is surprising how people can change positions when they are shown how the decision at hand fits into the values they have already ascribed to. Further, the team-building exercises you will use to build a trusting, caring climate will also support consensus. A further asset is that all your leaders will be trained in the consensus-building process—they will have skills they have not had before. A final aid is that all the team members know that consensus is expected and desirable. This is quite a change from the rugged individualism that is generally rewarded in our culture.

I could really identify with the stages of group development. It's clear to me that most of our groups are stuck at the membership or subgroup stages. I'm not clear how to get groups to the confrontation stage or how to get them through it. It seems like there could be a lot of bad feelings and that the group could just dissolve.

Three factors will help you get groups to move to the confrontational stage and then beyond. First, the members will now know that the decisions they make will really count, so they will have more of a vested interest in getting their positions on the table. Second, they will be participating in decision making on more substantive issues,

issues that really count with them. Third, they will know the stages of the group and will know that confrontation is one stage in the process—not pleasant, but necessary. As the group moves into the confrontation stage, it would be good to remind them from time to time that all are ascribing to the same values and the issue is how best to attain those values. In other words, help them keep their eyes on the target—help them see that they are making progress.

Implementation Checklist

_____ 1. A set of shared values is in place.

_____ 2. These shared values are the basis for all decision making in the district—budgets, staff development, curriculum, personnel, and so forth.

_____ 3. These shared values were developed through broad-based participation by board members, administrators, teachers, parents, students, and the community at large.

_____ 4. All decisions are made by consensus.

_____ 5. All school leaders understand the rationale for consensus and have discussed this with their subordinates.

_____ 6. All school leaders have been trained in various models for arriving at consensus and can use each at the appropriate time.

_____ 7. All school leaders have been trained to recognize the various stages of group development.

_____ 8. Peer observation teams have been formed to enable leaders to get peer feedback on their skills in consensus decision making and group development.

References

1. Einstein, Albert. 1954. *Ideas and Opinions*. New York, New York: Bonanza Books, p. 61.
2. Bock, Philip K. 1969. *Modern Cultural Anthropology*. New York, New York: Alfred A. Knopf, p. 367.
3. Bock, op. cit., p. 269.
4. Katz, Daniel and Robert L. Kahn. 1978. *The Social Psychology of Organizations*. New York, New York: John Wiley, p. 385.
5. Peters, Thomas J. and Robert H. Waterman. 1984. *In Search of Excellence*. New York, New York: Warner Books, p. 279.

6. Thompson, James D. 1967. *Organizations in Action.* New York, New York: McGraw-Hill, p. 127.

7. Katz and Kahn, op. cit., p. 385.

8. Ibid.

9. Goodlad, John I. et al. 1990. *The Moral Dimensions of Teaching.* San Fransisco: Jossey-Bass, p. 157.

10. Katz and Kahn, op. cit., p. 288.

11. Naisbitt, John and Patricia Aburdene. 1990. *Megatrends 2000.* New York, New York: William Morrow and Co., p. 298.

12. 1966. *Websters New World Dictionary.* Cleveland: The World Publishing Co., p. 312.

13. Pfeffer, Jeffrey. 1981. *Power in Organizations.* Marshfield Massachusetts: Pitman Publishing, Inc., p. 122.

14. Rist, Marilee C. 1989. "Here's What Empowerment Will Mean for Your Schools," *The Executive Educator* (August):17.

15. Lewis, Anne. 1989. *Restructuring America's Schools.* Arlington, Virginia: American Association of School Administrators, p. 71.

16. Duttweiler, Patricia Cloud. 1988. *Organizing for Excellence.* Austin, Texas: Southwest Educational Development Laboratory, p. 109.

17. Duttweiler, op. cit., p. 110.

18. Ohmae, Kenichi. 1984. *The Mind of the Strategist.* New York, New York: Penguin Books, p. 207.

19. Delbecq, Andre L., Andrew Van de Ven, David H. Gustafson. 1975. *Group Techniques for Program Planning.* Glenview, Illinois: Scott Foresman.

20. Delbecq, op. cit., p. 25.

21. Delbecq, op. cit., p. 18.

22. Lewis, James. 1985. *Excellent Organizations.* New York, New York: J. L. Wilkerson Co., p. 204.

23. Grunwald, Henry. 1990. *Time* (October):74.

24. Bradford, David L. and Allan R. Cohen. 1984. *Managing for Excellence.* New York, New York: John Wiley and Sons, pp. 170-203.

25. Cetron, Marvin and Owen Davies. 1989. *American Renaissance.* New York, New York: St. Martin Press, p. 362.

26. Hanson, Mark E. 1979. *Educational Administration and Organizational Behavior.* Boston: Allyn and Bacon, p. 100.

27. Robey, Daniel. 1982. *Designing Organizations: A Macro Perspective.* Homewood, Illinois: Richard D. Irwin, Inc., p. 347.

28. Weisbord, Marvin R. 1988. "Relationships," in *Team Building: Blue Prints for Productivity and Satisfaction.* W. Brendan Reddy, ed., NTL Institute for Applied Behavioral Science, p. 37.

29. Bradford and Cohen, loc. cit.

30. Bradford and Cohen, op. cit., p. 195.

31. Bradford and Cohen, op. cit., p. 188.

32. Ohmae, op. cit., p. 270.

33. Ohmae, op. cit., p. 273.

4 Guidelines for Restructuring

Restructuring is not merely an organizational principle (Chapter 1), an approach to leadership (Chapter 2), or the use of group processes (Chapter 3). It is all of these and more, for it consists of the total alignment of all aspects of the organization to achieve the purposes for which the organization was originally created. Marc Tucker [1] of the Carnegie Forum on Education and the Economy has said that very few aspects of restructuring are new in and of themselves, but rather the combining of them into a coordinated intervention is the essence of restructuring. Several key elements of restructuring, in addition to those presented in Chapters 1, 2, and 3, will be presented in this chapter. Each of these elements has been chosen for discussion due to its critical role in restructuring. None may be omitted, and most must be introduced simultaneously. This will not be as formidable as it might first appear since, as Marc Tucker has said, they are not really new.

Scientific Management, Human Relations, and Human Resources

Chapter 2 stressed the need for leaders in restructuring to be clear in their philosophy. A central aspect of that philosophy is clarity about the source of organizational improvement. In the scientific management view, experts are the source of organizational improvement. In such a framework it becomes the job of the leader to establish practice based on expert advice, to train subordinates to implement that practice, to monitor for compliance, and to retrain where necessary. No particular investment or commitment is necessary on the part of the subordinates since they are merely expected to comply with the process developed by the "experts." Much of the current school reform has been predicated on this view of change. It is reflected in required teaching processes loosely based on research, evaluations based on those specified processes, and advancement on a career ladder (or remediation/termination) based on conformity to those processes.

Human relations may be characterized as a "soft" scientific management. In this view, subordinates should be listened to and consulted. However, the purpose is not to change the processes, but rather to give the subordinate a good feeling about the organization and the processes. In this view the importance of subordinate investment and commitment is recognized; however, the ability of the subordinate to contribute substantially to the improvement of the process is not recognized. Teachers, parents, and others living in these conditions begin to feel frustration at the narrow range of opportunities for input they actually have. It is confusing because, on the surface, opportunities for contributions are available; however, nothing substantive seems to occur at the numerous meetings they attend. Human relations typically follows scientific management as a way of gaining the commitment and interest of the subordinates in making the processes derived by experts actually work. An important point here is that neither of these views involves any faith in the ability (and/or the interest) of the subordinate to improve his effectiveness on the job.

A different view of the source of organizational improvement has gained increasing influence in the past decade – human resources. As the name implies, the subordinates are seen as the real resources of the organization – human capital. Rather than being told what to do and how to do it, subordinates are expected to invent their jobs, as Kanter [2] puts it. Leadership for restructuring as described in Chapter 2 insures that the subordinates do not "invent" easy jobs for themselves. Being held to high moral goals and working in an environment that encourages risk and permits mistakes leads subordinates to high levels of commitment, creativity, and persistence.

Problems develop during a transition period in which elements of each of these views of organizational improvement are present in the same organization, leaving the members of the organization confused about the real expectations of the organization. Feeling the press of state mandates based on the scientific view of organizational improvement, wishing to soften that view somewhat by practicing some human relations, and reading the current management literature or feeling the press of the local union for more involvement, the school leader may fashion a confusing mix of compromises that leaves no one satisfied and does little to improve the productivity of the organization. It is critical, then, for school leaders to be clear about their fundamental commitments and to model these in decisions and practices.

Human Resources Organizations

Perhaps the best way to clarify human resources views is to contrast them with scientific management in some typical school functions. Under scientific management assumptions, teaching would be based on expert advice and would be highly specified. All teachers would be expected to follow the approved teaching process. No deviations would be permitted, since this would place the teacher at odds with expert advice. Under human resources assumptions, by contrast, teachers would be expected to reflect deeply about teaching and to develop their own unique styles and approaches in order to better serve their students. Differences between teachers would be expected; teachers might well meet in groups to enrich each other's thinking.

Teacher evaluation would also differ in scientific management and human resources. Under scientific management, the teacher would be evaluated with a uniform evaluation system based on the approved teaching practices. Under such a system, the students might not be doing well; still, the teacher could get a good evaluation and continue in the system, perhaps with an increase in rank. Under human resources management, teaching would be evaluated on the basis of what the teacher was trying to accomplish. Inevitably, various data sources would be used in order to gain information relevant to the purposes of the teacher. Student outcomes as measured by a variety of sources of data would be the primary focus, for if the teacher has the prerogative to select the teaching behaviors, the teacher also has the responsibility to vary those behaviors if the students aren't learning. Rather than being a "gotcha" approach to evaluation, human resources management would much more likely be a process for assisting teachers in reaching their goal of helping students learn.

Scientific management and human resources would also have a different approach to staff development or in-service. Scientific management would require the in-service needed to assist teachers in implementing the behaviors expected in the particular instructional approach to be specified. All teachers would attend the same in-service programs since all teachers would be expected to exhibit the same behaviors. Additional in-service opportunities would be provided for teachers who were not able to exhibit the behaviors. Human resources would be more likely to allow teachers to design their own in-service experiences. The options would be as wide as the variations in the teachers themselves.

From the above three examples, the differences between human resources and scientific management should be apparent. Many school districts currently display a mix of the two approaches, specifying certain flexible teaching behaviors–for example, giving some choice as to in-service–while simultaneously having a fairly uniform, standardized evaluation system. The mixed signals teachers receive tell them both that they are not professionals capable of exercising professional judgement and must therefore follow specified procedures, and that they *are* professionals capable of exercising choice! Faced with such conflicting messages, many teachers have expressed discouragement, according to the Second Gallup/Phi Delta Kappa Poll of Teachers' Attitudes [3], with more than half of them saying they have no substantive role in determining curriculum, discipline, or staff development.

In the absence of a consistent philosophy regarding the sources of organizational improvement, administrators may well be guilty of blaming the patient (teachers) instead of the disease (lack of an anchoring philosophy). In a recent survey of school administrators in West Texas, for example, the administrators identified morale as the top in-service need [4]; in effect, they were saying the patients (teachers) were the problem. Actually, informal conversations with teachers revealed that the organizational assumptions (the disease) were the *cause* of the low morale. Thus, the administrators were identifying a symptom rather than the problem, and recommending a remedy for the symptom. Then they expressed dismay when the remedy did not work! Not only must administrators have a clear view of the source of organizational improvement, they must also have an understanding of the intimate relationships between curriculum, instruction, and student discipline.

A Unified View of Curriculum, Instruction, and Discipline

Just as it is important for school leaders to have a clear view of the source of organizational improvement, it is also important for them to have a clear view of the relationship between curriculum, instruction, and discipline. If they do not, confusions similar to those discussed above can develop among teachers and students as a result of inconsistent decisions by administrators, which reveal conflicting views of the purposes of each of these elements.

The scientific management view will suggest one path to student learning; the human resources view will suggest quite another. For example, if the goal were to promote student thinking skills, the scientific management approach would be to locate a logically sequenced program recommended by experts, to have teachers move the students through it, and then to test for each skill as it was covered.

The result would be fragmented learning in which students emerge with bits and pieces of information but with little ability to apply the thinking skills to everyday problems.

Approached from the human resources view, the teacher would engage the *students* in solving a significant problem, and as the solution proceeded, the teacher might engage the students in Socratic dialogue that would press them on faulty assumptions, reaching illogical conclusions, ignoring evidence, and so forth. The same thinking skills would be covered, but in the context of solving real problems of concern to students. From such exercises, students would not necessarily learn the names of the thinking skills, but they would learn to use their minds to solve real-world problems, a thinking skill that should serve them well.

Turning to instructional practices, the scientific view would encourage teachers to be very active, dispensing information, making assignments, monitoring for compliance, issuing correctives, specifying how work was supposed to be completed, and so forth. Student learning would be verified by tests covering the material presented in class or assigned outside of class. By contrast, human resources would engage the *students* more actively in the learning process, focusing more on understanding and thinking, as Sizer's Coalition of Essential Schools [5] suggests, and less on content coverage.

Teaching for *understanding* can be increased by focusing on learning tactics in three categories: tactics for acquiring verbal knowledge, such as the facts fundamental to a subject (English, for example); tactics for acquiring procedural skills such as reading; and tactics for developing motivation [6]. Key tactics for increasing verbal learning include focusing (underlining, looking for headings, tables, italicized items), schema building (drawing a visual representation of the relationships between the various parts of the chapter in the book), and idea elaboration (encouraging students to link new information with prior knowledge). Key tactics for increasing procedural learning include hypothesizing (guessing why a particular pattern is or isn't an example of a concept), seeking reasons for actions (trying to determine which procedures are required in which situations), reflective self-instruction (comparing one's own performance with expert performance), and practice in part and later in entirety.

Key tactics for increasing motivation include behavioral self-management (breaking the task into subgoals and providing oneself with a reward as subgoals are attained), mood management (positive self-talk and using relaxation techniques), and self-monitoring (consciously stopping oneself in order to check mood, progress, etc.) This view of learning is generally in accordance with the work of Lauren

Resnick, co-director of the Learning Research and Development Center at the University of Pittsburgh [7] and David N. Perkins, Director of Project Zero at Harvard University [8], a project that is studying the various intelligences of humans. In the view of learning described above, the teacher would encourage group work, independent study, and interviews as instructional approaches and would use proposals, reports, demonstrations, exhibits, displays, and so forth to verify student learning.

Ron Brandt [9] has classified thinking emphases into three categories: teaching *for* thinking, teaching *of* thinking, and teaching *about* thinking. Brandt describes teaching *for* thinking as starting with intellectually engaging material (engaging for the student, not the teacher or the textbook author) and using teacher questioning, group discussion, and cooperative learning to deepen student engagement with the content. Teaching *of* thinking attempts to teach certain mental skills and processes (what we have discussed above under teaching for *understanding*). Teaching *about* thinking involves teaching students to consciously employ one of the thinking frames such as CoRT or Tactics for Thinking (see Appendix C). A consensus has developed around the idea that thinking skills should be integrated into the content, not taught as a separate subject. Someone has suggested that if the latter approach is taken, there is the great danger that thinking skills will become to learning what sentence diagramming has become to writing—a separate, isolated activity entirely detached from its original purpose.

Research into human cognition is far too rich and vibrant for detailed treatment in this section. The growth in this field may be illustrated by the fact that there are only thirteen entries in the ERIC system for the period 1976-1982 compared with 488 entries for the period 1983-1990 in the category Cognitive Process/Learning Strategies. One teacher or central office staff member might wish to become the district "expert," tracking the literature in this field. In order for this human resources view of learning and thinking to be successfully implemented, the student discipline policy would have to complement the implied view of students.

The scientific management approach to student discipline is perhaps best captured in Canter's Assertive Discipline Model [10]. In this approach, the expected behavior is specified, penalties for inappropriate behavior are established, and students are reinforced for good behavior. If a student accumulates enough bad marks, one of the penalties is invoked. This approach to discipline is compatible with the scientific management approach to learning described above, but it sends a message to students that is counterproductive for the kind of active, committed learning suggested by the human resources view. There is a message of trust in the human resources view of learning and discipline. Trust is simply not necessary in the scientific management view, because all of the learning and discipline is under the management of the teacher rather than the student. Since discipline and learning come from wholly external sources, why should students invest themselves?

This is the same question that teachers in a scientific management school ask. Thus, many students in such a school, Glasser suggests as many as 50 percent, do the minimum – if even that much – and ease their way through school. Glasser, on the other hand, proposes a different approach to student discipline.

In his book *Control Theory in the Classroom*, Glasser suggests that students will behave and try hard to do well in schools when they can see that their needs are being met. Needs fundamental to all individuals are needs for safety, love, power, fun, and freedom, according to Glasser [11]. In a school operating under scientific management, students respond with puzzlement when asked if any of their needs are being met. If pressed, they respond by naming extracurricular activities. Almost never, he reports, do students name an academic area in which their fundamental needs are being met. Most school administrators and the teachers in their schools are driven by the desire to raise standardized test scores, not to fashion school experiences that meet student needs. Since the students see little connection between what they are asked to learn and their immediate or future needs, they see little reason to invest themselves.

Glasser recommends that schools recast their role from test-score raising to designing programs that meet student needs. Such a program would ensure the safety of the student, assure him of his worth as an individual (love), permit participation in the design and content of the curriculum (power), provide opportunities for self-expression and cooperative learning (fun), and allow for varying patterns of achieving and verifying outcomes (freedom). In such a program there is little need for heavy emphasis on discipline because students do not resist a program that is meeting their needs. In instances where discipline is required, Glasser recommends a process developed from reality therapy: (1) become involved with the student personally, (2) confront the student with the reality of his/her role in the problem, (3) have the student develop a plan for solving the problem, and (4) get the student to commit to the plan. Glasser's process is much more involved than this brief discussion can permit; however, valuing of the individual as a human resource is as clear in this process as it is missing in assertive discipline where the control is external.

In summary, schools have, in the past, confused the basis upon which decisions were being made. In some instances, the decisions were based on scientific management views; then, in the same schools, other decisions were based on the human resources view. This confusion is not very surprising, for we have been in a transition period between these two views. Now, however, a sufficient consensus is developing that programs should begin to align their policies and decisions with human resources values in the critical areas of curriculum, instruction, and discipline.

Goals for Schools of the 21st Century

It is essential that school leaders create a sense of urgency if the full resources of the organization are to be mobilized in the coordinated change approach required by restructuring. Sufficient data exist to substantiate that educational productivity is at an unacceptable level:

- Motorola estimates that half its factory workers need remedial education just to attain seventh-grade math and English skills.
- In 1988, 44 percent of the job applicants at the Newark, NJ office of Prudential couldn't read at the ninth grade level.
- In 1987, BellSouth Corporation estimated that fewer than 10 percent of their job applicants met minimum requirements.
- A Fortune 500 company reported that it had to interview 600 applicants to hire sixty employees.
- The 1990 Wallchart published by the Department of Education reported declining scores on the SAT and ACT tests for the last three years. Former Secretary of Education Cavazos commented that it did not appear that the states had gotten serious about school reform.
- Using the Labor Department scale of 1-6 to rank the reading requirements of various jobs, authors of the report Workforce 2000 calculated that the 26 million jobs to be created between 1984 and 2000 will require a reading level of 3.6. Then using data from the National Assessment of Educational Progress, they calculated the reading level of the average young adult at 2.6. Commenting on these findings, Thomas Bailey, senior researcher at Columbia University, said we are witnessing the upskilling of jobs and the downskilling of the entering labor force.

- 750,000 students drop out of school every year. The test scores reported for high school students are those of our top students.
- America has 28 million illiterates; Japan has virtually none.
- Observers such as Glasser and Sizer suggest that as many as half of the students in school are "leaning on their shovels" most of the school day, while the teachers are working very hard.
- There is virtually unanimous agreement that the United States' economy is shifting from the Industrial Age to the Information Age. Even manufacturing jobs will require workers to process information.
- The Business Roundtable's Ad Hoc Committee on Education reports that, "As many as 60 percent of high school graduates are not prepared for entry-level jobs."
- John Goodlad has said that the problems of schooling are of such crippling proportions that many schools and even the entire public education system may not survive.
- *Training* magazine found in a survey of American companies employing over 10,000 workers that 30 percent were offering remedial education.
- The National Alliance of Businesses in a poll of business executives found that 64 percent were not satisfied with the reading, writing, and reasoning skills of high school graduates. Further, they found that 72 percent of the executives felt new employees' math skills had *worsened* between 1985 and 1990.
- A twenty-year summary of results of The National Assessment of Educational Progress reports virtually no improvement in achievement.

What has been the role of the schools in the past and how must that change in order to prepare students for the future? McNeil [12] and other educational historians have pictured the schools of the past as preparing workers for the routine of factory work. As such, the students were taught to deal with teacher-defined problems in a routine manner. They learned to work passively, quietly, at relatively uninteresting tasks for extended periods of time. They learned habits of orderliness, neatness, punctuality and obedience. Memorization, not thinking, was stressed. The system worked. American success and power became the standard of the world. As has been seen above, that system is not working anymore. Business can no longer find the workers it needs, for it needs a different kind of worker. The needs of business and the fact of the global economy have set a new agenda for schools:

- In a special section of *Business Week* Doyle [13] summarizes, "The modern economy – and the modern firm – needs broadly and deeply educated workers who can communicate with co-workers and customers, both verbally and in writing; workers who can solve problems and innovate, who can think critically and analytically, who can meet the public and deal with complex electronic technologies; workers who are alert and presentable and have a well-developed 'work ethic'; and most importantly, workers who are prepared to continue learning over their working lives."
- David T. Kearns [14], CEO of Xerox, opts for a liberal education for all students – "A liberal education not only imparts the great lessons of history, citizenship, and science, it teaches people to think, to solve problems, to take risks . . . to think independently, to step back from problems and the crowd, to be an entrepreneur and innovator. The virtues of a liberal education are the virtues of free enterprise in general and the high tech, knowledge-based society in particular: flexibility, adaptability, inventiveness, even playfulness."
- "Workforce 2000" [15] calls for change – "Students must go to school longer, study more, and pass more difficult tests covering more advanced subject matter. There is no excuse for vocational programs that 'warehouse' students who perform poorly in academic subjects or for diplomas that register nothing more than years of school attendance. From an economic standpoint, higher standards in the schools are the equivalent of competitiveness internationally."
- Taking its cue from the direct link between education, employment, and economic development, the Council of Chief State School Officers [16] sets the following goals for students: mastery of essential skills; foundation knowledge of our culture; self-discipline and creativity; thoughtful application of knowledge and skills to problems as a worker, family member, and citizen; caring involvement with others; and motivation for continuous learning. They further specify that graduates should have capacities for flexibility, diligence, competence, and responsibility. In a closing note they suggest that the learning environment

should reflect the characteristics that are the objectives of the instruction.

- The Education Commission of the States broadens the traditional definition of an educated individual by suggesting that states "develop a specific and demanding statement of what basic skills, thinking skills, knowledge, attitudes, and behaviors you (the states) want all students to have when they complete school. Student outcomes should meet employability criteria suggested by business and industry" [17].

Accountability of Schools, Teachers, and Parents

The calls for new definitions of learning, teaching, and student discipline, noted above, suggest that new standards of accountability must be forthcoming as well. While business and industry are calling for higher standards, they are not calling for more of the same – more memorized lists, more facts, more bits of fragmented information. The Information Age requires workers who can use information to frame and solve problems. It does not require memorizers or rule-followers. Presently used methods of accountability are under attack. The National Commission on Testing and the Public Policy [18] has stated, "Current testing, predominantly multiple choice in format, is over-relied upon, lacks adequate public accountability, sometimes leads to unfairness in the allocation of opportunities, and too often undermines vital social policies."

The weaknesses of the standardized tests currently used are evident from the assumptions upon which they rest. For example, in a typical item, students are asked to read a paragraph and select the most appropriate title from several listed. The presumption is that this tests the student's ability to grasp the central meaning of the paragraph. That, however, is not what is being tested. What is actually being tested is the ability of the student to correctly select from four choices, the one that most closely approximates the central meaning of the paragraph according to the writer of the four choices. Almost never in the real world will the student be asked to perform such a task.

Rather, a more real-world test of this skill would be to ask the student to actually write the meaning of the paragraph, or better yet, to ask the student to read the paragraph and take some action based on the meaning of the paragraph. This kind of test is variously called authentic assessment, real-world assessment, or performance assessment. The California Assessment Program is, perhaps, doing more than any other group at present to further the credibility of the authentic assessment. Grant Wiggins [19] suggests that we have gotten away from the meaning of a true test. According to Wiggins, a true test of intellectual ability requires the performance of exemplary tasks.

Dr. Ruth Mitchell [20] writing for *Beyond the Bubble* (a reference to the spaces that students "bubble-in" when answering standardized test questions), a conference sponsored by the California Assessment Program, says,

> Authentic assessment means evaluating by asking for the behavior you want to produce. If students should write well, ask them to write; if they should be able to solve problems using mathematical knowledge, ask them to do it. The principle applies in all curriculum areas; knowledge of a foreign language should mean being able to communicate, so test that. Knowledge of history and geography should mean understanding how it happened and what it means, so ask for those. Authentic assessment isn't a single method. It includes performance tests, such as conversations in a foreign language; observations; open-ended questions, where students tackle a problem but there's no single right answer; exhibitions in which students choose their own ways to demonstrate what they have learned; interviews; giving students a chance to reflect on their achievement; and portfolios, collections of student work. The list is limited only by the criterion of authenticity, "Is this what we want students to know and to be able to do?"

California State Superintendent of Education Bill Honig has said that rather than tell teachers statewide tests are important while at the same time telling them that they should not teach to the tests (!), they can now sidestep this conflict since the tests represent exactly what the state wants the students to know.

Authentic testing grows directly from the discussions of learning, teaching, and student discipline treated above, which is in line with knowledge for the Information Age. Several questions pose themselves.

Will the Public Accept These Tests?

The public can be prepared to accept these tests as one measure of student achievement during the broad-based community involvement activities described in Chapter 5. As the community comes to participate in defining the goals of education and as they grow in their understanding of requirements of workers in the 21st century, they will grow in their readiness to accept broader measures of student effectiveness. State-mandated test scores that are reported in the newspapers do attract much public attention. Again, the public can be prepared to accept the possibility of lower test scores as they come to understand the weaknesses of these tests and the fact that preparation for them absorbs an inordinate amount of instructional time with very little contribution to developing skills needed for the 21st century.

What Will Be the Costs of This Kind of Testing?

The cost for statewide authentic tests is about $15.00 per student compared to $5.00 per student for the machine-scored tests. In part the cost can be reduced by testing less often. However, since the tests point learning and instruction toward worthy goals, cost should be a minor consideration.

How Can Teachers Learn to Do This Kind of Testing in Their Classrooms?

A good source of information is the publication from the *Beyond the Bubble* conference, *A Sampler of Authentic Assessment*. One of the best methods, however, is for a group of teachers simply to subject their usual assignments or tests to the question, "Is this real-world?" For example, are book reports real-world? Is one ever required to read a book and write a report on it outside of a school situation? Personally I read dozens of books every year as a part of my job, yet I have never written a formal report on one. I read the books and take notes either to help me solve an issue I am currently pursuing, or I take notes for future reference. But I never write a formal report. Taken to its limit, this kind of questioning might eliminate most tests because in the real world we do not take tests as a regular part of our responsibilities. Teacher acceptance of authentic assessment may be more difficult than their learning how to do it. Public acceptance will help speed teacher acceptance.

Will Students Study and Learn If Authentic Assessment Is Utilized?

The answer to this question is a definite "Yes." While there will likely be less storage in short-term memory (e.g., cramming for tests), since students are studying topics about which they deeply care, there is likely to be more learning. Writing in the *Business Week* supplement "Endangered Species: Children of Promise," Doyle [21] states,

> As John Dewey argued at the turn of the century, the job of the school is to prepare children for a fulfilling life in a democratic society: Educate "the whole child." Such an approach can finally be a reality, because the individual educated for work is also educated for life.

This is a goal that schools, teachers and the public have not embraced in the past; however, it is the goal being articulated by the business community in preparation for the 21st century.

How Will Students Do on Such Accepted Measures of Student Achievement as the Scholastic Aptitude Tests?

Students who have attended schools that are members of Sizer's Coalition of Essential Schools have not noted a decrease in scores on standardized measures. Test publishers, sensitive to the charges that their tests have promoted fragmented teaching, are already working on tests that are more authentic or performance-based. The minimum skills tests that were mandated by many states as a part of the education reform movement of the 1980s are already being upgraded to require more of the kinds of skills tested in authentic tests.

Will This Kind of Testing Prepare Students for the 21st Century?

Workers of the 21st century, the Information Age, will be expected to monitor the environment for problems, frame these in some fashion that is relevant to the goals of the organization, and utilize information to solve them. They will be working in teams and will assign themselves tasks in order to achieve the goals of the organization, goals that they have helped establish. In short, they will be engaging in the very activities that authentic assessment promotes in the classroom. Yes, students should be very well prepared to work in 21st century organizations.

How Will Students Who Are Authentically Assessed Do in College?

They should do well. Much of college involves working independently in a self-disciplined way to achieve the goals of the course. Authentic assessment does not mean lower standards; rather, students are much more likely to work hard on tasks that are of interest to them as opposed to teacher-set tasks. Indeed, college itself will be compelled by the same forces that are impacting on the public schools to change from the lecture-dominated format most of us remember.

Reflecting on the university of the future, the Commission on the University of the 21st Century [22] projects that most students will attend fewer lectures and those they do attend will be televised; they will access reference materials from their rooms via a terminal; they will meet informally with faculty members for discussions and reflection. Not only will the means of instruction change, but the focus will change as well with more emphasis on analysis and integration and less emphasis on memorization of facts.

Summary

Scientific management has dominated leadership practices for much of the 20th century. It has focused on efficiency and has largely ignored the human factor in leadership. While it was effective under the prevailing culture, it is no longer serving organizations well. Human relations was an attempt to introduce the human factor into the management process while still retaining the central tenets of scientific management. Human relations managers were more considerate of the employees and tried to make them feel good about themselves and the organization by giving them some opportunity to voice an opinion. Their opinions, however, either carried little weight or were only solicited on minor issues.

By contrast, human resources leadership recognizes the central importance of employees and includes them in key decisions of the organization. Far from an experimental approach, human resources represents the best practice of some of the major corporations.

At the end of the 20th century we find ourselves in a transitional period, with a mixture of both scientific management and human resources being practiced in the same organization, often by the same leader! This sends a mixed and confusing signal to employees: "We value your input, but do things this way because this is the best way." Restructuring rests heavily on human resources concepts; therefore, any attempt to restructure an organization must be guided by a clear commitment to align all organizational practices—in schools this means instruction, curriculum, and student discipline—with human resources leadership.

Instruction must shift from the scientific management view of the teacher as dispenser of information to that of the teacher as a facilitator of learning. Curriculum must shift from the orderly presentation of lists, a scientific management view, to broader concepts in which students can engage deeply. Student discipline must shift from a reward and punishment emphasis to a problem-solving attitude.

These changes will necessitate a shift in assessment processes. There will be fewer tests of facts and more authentic assessments — assessments that require students to exhibit learning in a real-world context. That is, if the assessment is something that is only practiced in a school setting, it will be eliminated in favor of an assessment that more nearly reflects a real-world expectation. Students should do better work under the emergent views since these are in line with a developing cultural and business ethos. School leaders can assist the public in accepting these emergent views through such activities as the broad community participation described in Chapter 5.

Troubleshooting

Our writing scores are down at the elementary school level. I am thinking about recommending a writing program I heard about at the state conference of superintendents. How could I do this from a human resources approach?

It sounds like you already have your mind made up. If this is true, you don't need a human resources approach. Just mandate it from the top down. However, don't be surprised if the teachers don't deeply commit themselves to it. If you really wished to take a human resources approach, a lot of work would have preceded the decision on how to improve writing in the elementary school (see Chapter 5). Assuming that work has been done, you might pose the question of improvement of writing skills to the elementary teachers (or better yet, have the principals do this). Through collaboration with teachers and perhaps involving parents and businessmen, a program will be fashioned to which the teachers can feel a deep commitment. It is this deep commitment by teachers and parents that can make a program successful. Guard against the traditional approach whereby teachers simply adopt a canned program, since this will not develop the ownership required for long-term improvement in writing. Encourage research as a basis for program development. Be ready to offer financial support if this is necessary. Even a small budget can send a signal that "this is important."

How can you get teachers to lecture less and have more student involvement in learning? I have tried everything and still most teachers do most of the talking most of the time.

You seem to be making a top-down decision that lecture is in and of itself a bad thing. Rather than approaching the problem that way, which is to say maintaining a scientific management approach, you might make the research on human cognition available to teachers, form them into teams, and encourage them to review different teaching options. They might gather data on their own teaching to see if they are utilizing the best we know about human cognition. Another approach might be to suggest the teachers set aside one day a week to experiment with another teaching style, and that they form discussion groups to debrief each other on the fit between their lesson and the process of human cognition. Basically, a cultural norm has developed in many schools that prevents teachers from experimenting for fear of making a mistake. That norm has to be changed to an expectation that teachers will constantly experiment on better ways of teaching, with student outcomes the measure of success.

One of the goals adopted from the community involvement described in Chapter 5 might be that teachers utilize the best and most recent research in their effort to help each student experience academic success. Another goal that could grow from community involvement might be that educational experiences will assist students in developing the skills needed to be successful in the 21st century. Since two of those skills are problem-framing and working as part of a team, teachers might measure the effectiveness of their usual methods of instruction in terms of that goal. Some teachers have achieved personal gratification by teaching to top students in a lecture format. They must be pressed to measure their effectiveness with respect to all of the goals of the school, not merely with respect to the conventional academic goals (lists of information) and only with students who learn these lists by passively listening.

How can I help my teachers understand and use authentic assessment?

As teachers study the emergent research on human cognition, they will come to see that much of what they have been teaching and testing has been stored in short-term memory. As they grow in their understanding, they should begin to raise questions about their teaching and testing practices (again, as in the previous answer, assuming that the base of community support as described in Chapter 5 has been built). Practices similar to those suggested in the previous answer should assist the school leader in altering the culture of teaching to, and testing for, the information in short-term memory. A chart and some sample authentic test items have been included in Appendix D to assist understanding of this approach to verifying student learning.

I anticipate a lot of teacher resistance to much of what you have proposed in this chapter. In a sense you are suggesting that many of the standard practices in classrooms are bad. Yet in our district, conventional teaching has produced university scholarships, community pride, winners in state-level academic competitions, and so forth. By and large, most of the community is satisfied with the education the students are receiving. Many of our teachers have been praised for their teaching effectiveness. By emphasizing the negatives as you have in this chapter, I think the teachers would either be highly resistant or their morale would drop to zero.

That could certainly be one outcome. Change is rarely smooth and those who have to change the most are good bets to squawk the loudest. There is no doubt that many good scholars have emerged from the best of conventional teaching. However, by starting with a solid base of community understanding and support as described in Chapter 5 and exercising the leadership described in Chapter 2, the recognition of the need for change and the willingness to risk change can be nurtured. Much support must be given to teachers during this period, particularly those teachers who are trying new approaches. If you do not feel that your situation will permit all schools in your district or even all teachers in one building to move in the direction of change at the same time, let a few buildings or teachers serve as the vanguard. The others should know, however, that they will be expected to follow, and the rewards and recognitions should flow to the vanguard teachers or buildings. A plan for starting with just a few schools is presented in Appendix K. Further, teachers and buildings should know that no particular practices are expected; rather a variety of practices will likely emerge as teachers try different behaviors, evaluate the outcomes, receive feedback from a peer team, reflect on their experiences, and modify accordingly.

Implementation Checklist

_____ 1. Teachers and building principals have accepted excellence as the standard they strive for.

_____ 2. All professional staff have accepted that all students can learn.

_____ 3. All professional staff have accepted that they control the essential factors in learning.

_____ 4. Teachers and building principals have examined the district data regarding student performance and accept the need for improvement.

_____ 5. All professional staff recognize that doing more of the same is not likely to produce significant gains in pupil learning.

_____ 6. All professional staff understand that there is not likely to be a perfect learning program out there just waiting to be discovered.

_____ 7. Related to #6 above, all professional staff accept that the answers to improved instruction likely lie within themselves as they read research, reflect on their own experiences, and consider the unique context of their teaching environment.

_____ 8. Improvement study teams have been formed to implement #7 above.

_____ 9. An expectation that all staff will improve has been established.

_____ 10. Curricula, instructional practices, assessment practices, and student discipline policies have been examined for a uniform view (e.g., the human resource view).

_____ 11. Support for risk-taking is a clear priority for the district.

_____ 12. Recognition has been provided for buildings, teams, or individual teachers who are trying to implement the understandings they have gained from research.

_____ 13. Students, parents, and the community have been kept informed of the change in educational practices and the students have been assisted in learning their new role expectations.

_____ 14. Professional staff, students, parents, and the community have accepted as valid the goal of enabling students to develop the skills and understandings required for success in the 21st century.

_____ 15. Professional staff are sufficiently knowledgeable in the areas of human resource development, human cognition, and the curriculum and instructional practices implied by our understanding of human cognition, so that they are able to discuss these with parents and community members.

References

1. O'Neil, J. 1990. "Piecing Together the Restructuring Puzzle," *Education Leadership*, 47:4-10.

2. Kanter, M. 1983. *Change Masters*. New York: Simon and Schuster.

3. Elam, S. 1989. "The Second Gallup/Phi Delta Kappa Poll of Teachers' Attitudes Toward the Public Schools," *Phi Delta Kappan*, 70:785-798.

4. Reavis, C. "Teacher In-Service Needs," an unpublished survey of area school administrators.

5. Sizer, T. 1988. "Interview with Ron Brandt," *Educational Leadership*, 45:22-24.

6. Derry, S. 1988/1989. "Putting Learning Strategies to Work," *Educational Leadership*, 46:4-10.

7. Resnick, L. 1987. *Education and Learning to Think*. Washington, D.C.: Academic Press.

8. Perkins, D. 1990. "On Knowledge and Cognitive Skills: A Conversation with David Perkins," *Educational Leadership*, 47:50-53.

9. Brandt, R. 1988. "Two Possibilities," *Educational Leadership*, 45:3.

10. Canter, L. 1976. *Assertive Discipline: A Take Charge Approach for Today's Educator.* Santa Monica, CA: Lee Canter and Associates.

11. Gough, P. 1987. "The Key to Improving Schools: An Interview with William Glasser," *Phi Delta Kappan*, 68:656-662.

12. McNeil, L. 1986. *Contradictions of Control.* London: Rautledge and Kagan Paul.

13. Doyle, D. 1989. "Endangered Species: Children of Promise," *Business Week*, Special Supplement:22.

14. Kearns, D. 1989. "Endangered Species: Children of Promise," *Business Week*, Special Supplement:24.

15. Johnson, W. 1987. "Workforce 2000: Work and Workers for the Twenty-First Century," U.S. Department of Labor Research Report No. HI-3796-RR, p. xxvii.

16. Council of Chief State School Officers. 1989. *Success for All in the New Century.* Washington, D.C.: The Council.

17. Education Commission of the States. 1990. "A Roadmap for Restructuring Schools," *Education Week* (March):24.

18. National Commission on Testing and the Public Policy. 1990. *From Gatekeeper to Gateway: Transforming Testing in America.* Chestnut Hill, MA: The Commission.

19. Wiggins, G. 1989. "A True Test: Toward More Authentic and Equitable Assessment," *Phi Delta Kappan*, 70: 703-713.

20. Mitchell, R. 1989. "A Sampler of Authentic Assessments," from *Beyond the Bubble*, 1989 Curriculum/Assessment Alignment Conferences, Long Beach, CA, (October 29-31, 1989), p. 3.

21. Doyle, D. op. cit., p. 24.

22. Commission on the University of the 21st Century. 1989. *The Case for Change.* Richmond, VA: The Commission.

⑤ Building Support

This is not a time to report to you that we need to make a timid, pilot-scale, tip-toeing into new waters approach to electronic education... Rather, this is a time for total immersion. Our children's education is not a game, but the football analogy is that we are in the fourth quarter with no time-outs, and we are behind!

PAMPA 2000 CHAIRMAN

School reform efforts of the 1980s have consistently overlooked the importance of authentic partnership between schools and parents, businessmen and other citizens in the improvement of local public education. Every year, school officials, teachers, club sponsors, and activity directors ask their community for financial support through tax drives, adopt-a-school programs, and endless candy sales and car washes. While the average citizen of most communities in America is supportive of these efforts, what role does he or she have in making real decisions for improvement of schools? And is there a way to mobilize the average citizen to join teachers in the improvement of the quality of education for their children? The answer from a conservative Texas Panhandle community of 20,000 citizens and 4,300 children appears to be, yes!

Between 1987 and 1989, the Pampa school board initiated three citizen task forces, composed of seventeen committees and hundreds of citizens, to trigger what has now become a remarkable new era in school-community design for improved school performance. The quote at the start of this chapter was made by one committee chairman as he addressed the Pampa school board following months of investigation into advanced technologies for public school classrooms. Scores of local businessmen and parents united with dozens of volunteer school personnel and board members to make a set of aggressive recommendations that would impact a dozen areas of the Pampa school program. The community-based initiatives created a redesign of numerous programs: honors courses, plans for improving student self-esteem, reducing the dropout rate, addressing student study skills, redesigning staff training, and a host of other important areas.

The total community effort boosted school district costs by more than $1.5 million and raised the local tax rate by approximately 20 percent—all with widespread community support—unprecedented for a school district with a $14 million budget.

A case in point was the Task Force on Computer Technology. The Computer Task Force recommended the installation of satellite technology for professional training, the expansion of systemwide classroom video use and, most significantly, an increase in the number of classroom computers from a ratio of 1 to 43 to 1 to 11 students over a two-year period. This kind of school initiative would have been impossible without widespread community involvement. Most importantly, lay members of the community were working in concert with teachers and other school personnel both in making decisions for substantive school restructuring and seeing that these initiatives were successfully carried out. This process is beginning to have a dramatic impact on the quality of education for every child in the Pampa school district. The remainder of this chapter will focus on processes and techniques for generating a restructuring of public school education.

Creating an Effective Loose-Tight Organization

Many researchers and practitioners alike refer to restructuring as the shifting of responsibility for making decisions from the central office to the schoolhouse. Instead of narrowly limiting the authority for making decisions through centrally controlled bureaucratic methods, it is argued that teachers and principals must have the power to be more adaptive and flexible in their schools. Thus, those closest to the job are recognized as the experts for making decisions about organization, personnel, structure, methods, and the allocation of resources. This sounds good. In fact, this *is* good, but is there more to restructuring? Is restructuring really just a territorial battle between the advocates of the entrenched bureaucracy and the advocates of site-based management? The answer is no! Genuine restructuring for improved school results is neither a top-down nor a bottom-up decision-making process—it is both! It is both tight at the strategic level and loose at the operational level, but most of all it is collaborative at both levels between the school board, teachers, parents, and citizens of the community.

Peters and Waterman [1] describe the loose-tight nature of some of America's most successful corporations. Companies like 3M, Texas Instruments, and McDonald's are characterized as having rigid organizational controls, "yet at the same time allow (indeed, insist on) autonomy, entrepreneurship, and innovation from the rank and file." This seeming paradox is the equivalent of "having one's cake and eating it too," as strong direction comes from the top while individuality is vigorously promoted throughout all levels of the organization. How can the top and bottom operate in a state of effective communication and cooperation under these conditions? Is it really possible for both educators and lay citizens to co-partner in remaking the educational programs of our schools? The process is difficult, but let's review some of the proven steps for building support at all levels of a school system and from throughout the community for improved student performance. The steps can be divided into two phases: identifying a need and clarifying a response.

Identifying a Need

Internal and External Data Collection: Honesty Is the Best Policy

In the fall of 1987, district leaders began an introspective investigation into how students were doing. They knew they could not build support for improved school results without creating and disseminating a data base on how students were doing at all levels of the school system. Thus, records on student test scores were disaggregated, dropout rates were identified, and grades and school failures were analyzed. Additional information was gathered from counseling files and local service agencies on aspects of suicide, mental depression, pregnancy, chemical abuse, and other forms of physical and mental abuse among youth of all ages. This type of information can be a surprise (if not a real shock) when first introduced throughout a school system and must be continually presented in an objective, positive, and supportive manner.

It is often difficult to be forthright and honest about the failures of children without either being obsessively defensive or resorting to blaming conditions beyond the control of schools. After all, deception over student failure is rarely intentional. As Bradford and Cohen [2] have emphasized, "conditioning the turf" is an extremely important factor in building readiness for changes that could affect an individual's work. In many school organizations—and the Pampa district was no exception—the scrutinization of student data is very threatening to staff who feel unsupported or are unfamiliar with analyzing many sources of information. After all, this information can require changes in habits, interdependencies, and methods for performing. In order to reduce anxieties and condition the staff for receptiveness to change, school leaders assigned small ad hoc groups to review and analyze student data.

After months of study this group reached several conclusions: almost 20 percent of all elementary students had been retained at least once, 26 percent of all entering ninth grade students were overage, 29 percent of all high school students were two or more years behind grade level in reading or math, and 16 percent of the high school students were 3.5 years behind grade level. The analysis further revealed that each senior class over the past decade was a full one-third smaller than when its members were freshmen. To compound these findings, a study of teaching conditions revealed that the recent decline in the Texas oil economy had left Pampa teachers severely short of supplies, equipment, and training. Despite the fact that the reaction to this information varied from immediate acceptance to complete rejection, it nevertheless presented an imperative for change and provided a context for contemplating changes in the school district.

This information was communicated to small groups of school personnel and numerous community civic groups. By June 1988, a widespread conviction had developed that school practices and programs had to change. The leadership group followed the internal study with an external analysis of the local economy. The Pampa community lies in the middle of a large oil and gas field that for decades provided well-paying jobs to thousands of area oil field workers–employment opportunities that rapidly disappeared during the 1980s. Very few oil field jobs required a high school diploma, and expectations for graduation were traditionally low among many of the working class families of Pampa, a condition that is similar to hundreds of communities across America with a manufacturing or natural resource based economy. On the positive side, a large Celanese chemical plant in the community provided encouragement and intellectual support for an educated work force. As a result of the analysis, a widespread conviction had developed that significant action on behalf of every child had to occur.

Clarifying a Response

Building Momentum from the Bottom up and Outside In

> *This process requires creative thinking. . . . One must be able to think in large expanding concentric circles on a pond. . . . Some seemed to have an ability to think to the distance of only one ripple, while others could see to the last ripple touching the shore. . . . It seemed to be a*

natural way to think for some, and perhaps it can be taught, but it was difficult for many of us to imagine past our own experience. This is why interaction through the Pampa 2000 project was so important between the businessman, parent, second grade teacher and school board member. The sphere of experience was different for each . . . and everyone was challenged to see the whole picture.

CHAIRMAN AND PARENT VOLUNTEER

From the very beginning, school leaders in the Pampa District systematically worked to involve the school board, principals, teachers, and a wide variety of citizens from the community. They conducted numerous board, administrator, and faculty workshops and retreats where student information was discussed and analyzed. In every gathering they were very careful to include a balanced mix of top administrative staff, mid-managers, teachers, and leaders from throughout the community. By the summer of 1988, the school leadership and board were convinced that the entire community could be mobilized for school improvement. This broad-based community support was critical to sustain any major changes. At the same time, revealing the extent of the school problems carried a substantial risk to the school administration and board. The risk of being honest about the lack of student success can vary from a loss of prestige by well-trained staff to eruptions of infighting between political factions within a community.

For these and many other reasons, school administrators and school boards are sensitive — often resistant — to revealing the true nature of failure by school children. Teachers feel unsupported and distant from the decision-making process in discussing student failure. Administrators feel compelled to put the best face on student performance as a way to protect themselves from the political repercussions of poor student performance. For example, the typical central office staff report on student test scores is constructed by averaging the test results of an entire grade level, when in fact the grade level average disguises the performance of students at the bottom half of the average. The bottom half of the average often includes hundreds, thousands, and on a larger scale millions of low-performing children of every age group. The same is true when trying to determine a school dropout rate. Until recently very few school systems even bothered to collect this information, and many continue to ignore the large population that leaves school during the summer months when school is out of session.

There is enormous pressure within a school system to gloss over the realities of student failure. In an era of accountability for improvement in test scores, administrators are quick to rationalize student failure as an inevitability; similarly, they are tempted to dismiss student failure since it is they who directly feel the scorn of the community when the lack of success by low-performing students is openly discussed. Facing this type of criticism, teachers understandably become defensive and divisive. In a work environment that is highly segmented among teachers, between grade levels, and across job descriptions, the risks for being honest about student failure are enormous.

The Pampa school district was confident that the risks for being honest over student performance could be minimized with a bottom-up and outside-in design. The charge to each organized group included planning activities for both the strategic and operational levels of the school district. No limits were set on participation at either level, as all planning activities were to be conducted with a bottom-up and outside-in design. School leaders recognized that too often teachers are left out of the central direction-setting process, and, in fact, direction setting is usually mandated from the top down. It was determined that all future planning efforts would mesh from the bottom up. Similarly, lay citizens are frequently asked for input, but rarely do they share in making and monitoring substantive decisions for school operations. This was to be a community planning program that would be integrated from the outside in.

To achieve bottom-up and outside-in success, teachers were encouraged to participate in the unfamiliar role of policymaker at the strategic level, while board members and top staff also could share in any decisions at the operational level. To clarify how this worked, a board member might join in developing a campus operational plan for improving self-esteem among seventh grade students, and in a similar vein, a teacher might join in making districtwide recommendations initiating a costly K-12 computer education program. Thus, a person was not limited in his contributions merely by the nature of the role he filled in the organization. This bottom-up and outside-in planning allowed the district to gain momentum in its project for improved student results.

To establish a workable process for each committee, there were two rules that could not be violated. First, the committees would commit to being representative of all citizen and teacher groups. As a corollary to that rule, no person of "ill will" would be allowed to participate. Ill will did not refer to critics, skeptics, or individuals with deep concerns about public education – all of whom were in fact encouraged to join – but rather it referred to those few individuals who would seek to destroy any group regardless of expertise or objective information. And second, expertise and knowledge were to be the principle bases for power and influence in each group, rather than position or authority. These two rules were incorporated into the training of each committee, and they helped to guide and assure maximum success for their proceedings.

Pampa 2000 Framework

A joint meeting with the local Industrial Foundation board of directors, City of Pampa council members, and representatives of the county government was used to gain general acceptance for a school district planning project that was eventually to be called "Pampa 2000." Following this meeting in June 1988, the school board formally inaugurated Pampa 2000 as the most detailed and complete planning project in the history of the community. In virtually every case, members of the school board volunteered to either chair or assume an active working role with each task force and many of the appointed committees. This bold proposal had a highly energizing effect on both the professional school staff and the community.

Over the next twelve months the school board authorized three major task forces with a total of seventeen working committees. The three task forces were assigned the responsibility of designing plans for at-risk youth, computer technology use, and other targeted or strategic areas (see Figure 1). The Pampa school board and school administrators first worked to identify a set of tasks that had to be accomplished before the task forces could proceed:

- Define the purpose of each task force, that is, what is to be accomplished.
- Develop general rules of operation for the task forces and all committees.
- Set timetables for the task forces and the committees within each task force.
- Develop the method of selection to each task force.

Once these tasks were completed, the At-Risk and Computer Technology Task Forces used a process for creating a common *vision* for better schools, while the Strategic Planning Task Force used a slightly different orientation—a *mission* process—for generating a widespread commitment to school improvement. In addition, the members of the Strategic Planning Task Force met annually to review these plans. Thus, the Strategic Planning Task Force included an audit feature that was to check the effectiveness of all plans as they became imbedded into the total school program. Each of the three task forces was expected to make recommendations to the school board for im-

PAMPA 2000

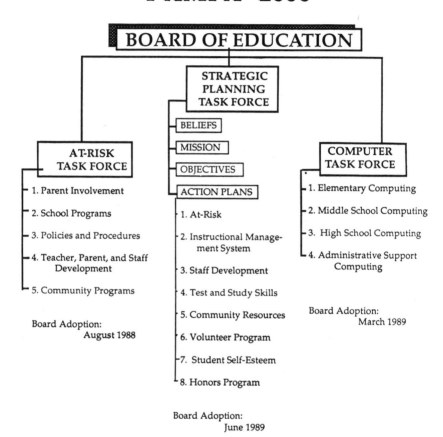

BOARD OF EDUCATION

STRATEGIC PLANNING TASK FORCE

BELIEFS
MISSION
OBJECTIVES
ACTION PLANS

AT-RISK TASK FORCE

1. Parent Involvement
2. School Programs
3. Policies and Procedures
4. Teacher, Parent, and Staff Development
5. Community Programs

Board Adoption:
August 1988

1. At-Risk
2. Instructional Management System
3. Staff Development
4. Test and Study Skills
5. Community Resources
6. Volunteer Program
7. Student Self-Esteem
8. Honors Program

Board Adoption:
June 1989

COMPUTER TASK FORCE

1. Elementary Computing
2. Middle School Computing
3. High School Computing
4. Administrative Support Computing

Board Adoption:
March 1989

P.I.S.D
Success for one -
Success for all!

FIGURE 1.

100

proved school programs. A single set of baseline expectations was established for each group:

- They were expected to have a considerable amount of input from both within and outside the school district.
- They were to operate in a participatory manner using the rules of consensus for making decisions (see Chapter 3).
- They were to have ways to measure the success of the goals or at least make suggestions for "first steps."

Guided by these expectations, the Pampa 2000 project was able to succeed with the two distinctly different approaches for arriving at expected outcomes—the visions approach and the mission approach. Each approach has its own unique set of operations, characteristics, strengths, and weaknesses. It cannot be emphasized enough that while both approaches are distinctly different in process, the end results or products for each process have been very similar. Each task force has created a districtwide integrated wave for change that continues to show promise for guiding the Pampa school district onto the path of continuous school improvement for years to come.

Building Vision

Corporate America functions best when it develops a vision, determines priorities and strategies, builds consensus, provides leadership and addresses, with all available resources, whatever thorny challenge lies in its path. [3]

The idea of planning for the future of the Pampa schools was wrapped up in change—not random or accidental change, but intentional change that was based on where the citizens of Pampa wanted their schools to be. For this to happen it was necessary to realize that the existing roadmap of school practices and traditions could be reconstructed to guide the school district into improved school performance. Early on it was decided that the process was not going to be a detailed community blueprint for the resolution of every single problem in the schools. Further, it was realized that two pictures needed to be drawn about the Pampa school district. The first picture would be a visualization of the ideal schools for Pampa—the schools that the Pampa community most wanted to have. The second picture of Pampa would be an objective and accurate description of the schools as they currently exist. Then the community- and teacher-based planning teams could decide if the status quo was what they wanted or if indeed there was room for change.

In July through October 1988, the At-Risk and Computer Education Task Forces were formed to initiate the Pampa 2000 project. Each task force followed the "vision" approach by describing the ideal and the current pictures of Pampa schools. Members of the task forces were appointed through advertisements, board solicitation, and volunteer drives. The task force chairmen were appointed from the school board, while committee chairs were selected from the total volunteer pool, and training sessions were conducted by district administrators for each task force. The training sessions were designed to achieve three major outcomes—genuine teamwork, subject familiarity, and visioning for better schools.

Genuine Teamwork

The initial training session stressed the importance of teamwork through a group of team-building exercises. First, it was important for each member of the task force to get to know each other as individuals from different parts of the community. Various "get to know you" exercises were systematically used to accomplish this purpose. Second, it was necessary that they understand the unique perspective that each member brought to the task force. Thus, members of the task forces were asked to share their schooling experiences with team-building exercises like: "The best thing I liked about my favorite teacher in elementary school was . . ." or, "My best friend in high school helped me by. . . ." These exercises were successful in fostering teamwork and commitment throughout and beyond the life of each task force committee.

Subject Familiarity

The members of each committee were asked to participate in a series of fact-finding investigations in the area of their assignment. Following initial fact-oriented presentations by school district staff, committee members visited Pampa schools, visited other school districts, reviewed relevant literature, and interviewed personnel both inside and outside of the school district. In general, each committee conducted an inventory and analysis of existing school district conditions. Each committee was given materials and an organizing notebook and was supported with secretarial help. By the time they were finished with this process, most of the members of every committee were very familiar with the subject matter of their assignment.

Visioning for Better Schools

The vision approach to school improvement necessitated that each committee work together to imagine what their schools should be like in the year 2000. The process of re-creating existing conditions for the success of all children is not easy for many people – in particular, for teachers and staff directly involved in a committee area. For instance, it may be difficult for a Chapter 1 teacher to envision the elimination of pull-out programs when that teacher has worked for many years only in pull-out programs. Likewise, a principal may have a difficult time envisioning a leadership council of teachers when his or her experience has been that we get our "marching orders" from the central office. A parent may have a difficult time envisioning a restructured high school because of limited experience with schools.

The committees of each task force were asked to follow a four-step vision-building process:

(1) Describe the ideal that you imagine for your committee assignment by the year 2000.
(2) What is the current status? What programs are in place? How effective is each program?
(3) What are the gaps between the current situation and the ideal for the year 2000?
(4) What are some methods, or at least some suggested first steps, to close the gap?

It has been mentioned that it is hard for many individuals to envision better programs for the future, but the most significant pitfall of the visioning approach was with the use of the term *gap*. While many school district employees worked efficiently with this type of process, there were a number of teachers and staff who took the word *gap* very personally. If there was perceived to be a gap between "what is" and "what could be," then they became defensive, as they felt their current practices were on trial – with the implication that they were at fault. This was readily apparent to many parents and businessmen from the community. As one parent commented, she regularly heard, "Oh, we're already doing this" when the feeling she had was that it was not being done, and that the idea for change was in danger of being shelved. Thus, it was extremely important that many citizens fully participate in all proceedings in order to press school personnel toward change. Yet, it remained correspondingly important to school leaders to gently remind everyone that this was a program review and not a reflection of any school employee's work.

Collectively, the recommendations of the At-Risk and Computer Technology Task Forces were compiled into a manual for school board examination. The linkage between the task forces and school board were strengthened by the fact that each task force was chaired by a school board member. As one board member commented, "It was a real challenge striving to make productive volunteers of former critics." When asked about the strength of this school-community design, one of the school board members summarized her thoughts by saying, "The challenge of drawing together different people of the community of different races, religions, and socioeconomic groups was gratifying. Seeing them become a viable work force with an identified well-defined task was a rare opportunity for our district to grow."

The At-Risk and Computer Technology Task Forces, led by three school board members, were divided respectively into five and four working committees. The committees were chaired by volunteer teachers, administrators, parents, and businessmen, and they varied in size from eight to sixteen members. In each committee a strong mix of parent, teacher, administrator and businessman was maintained. The meetings for every committee were under the direction of the individual chairman. It was the responsibility of the chairman to call and organize the agenda for each committee meeting. The chairman was to follow the vision outline by developing a written description of outcomes for the schools, to examine current programs for any gaps, and, finally, to make recommendations for goals and objectives for school improvement.

Because the strength of the committee depends on the success or failure of the committee chairman, the task force leader would call weekly meetings of his/her respective chairs to share problems or provide technical support as needed. Frequently, the superintendent and other central office administrators would attend these particular meetings to interpret technical information, to provide clarification, or to respond to any questions on existing services or future plans. Often the chairmen would have technical questions about the nature of their areas or about the level of specificity in setting goals and objectives. At times these meetings were a good way to vent frustration over the operation of their committees or to simply provide an opportunity to learn from the experiences of other chairs.

It was anticipated that many issues would emerge in the visioning work of each committee. Thus, a set of "rules for consensus" was adopted for the internal decision making of each committee. The rules of consensus, adopted to conform to a participatory style of group leadership, were quite simple but effective. The first rule of consensus was "everyone participates." In the complicated field of learning and teaching it is often a reality that the person of greatest position in the school organization has the most to say—regardless of expertise. In addition, in every group there are a few who will naturally tend to dominate, while there are a few who will be very quiet during the proceedings. Thus, the importance of icebreakers and team-building (see Chapter 3) exercises for small group success cannot be overstated. The second rule of consensus pertains to the effective use of brainstorming and clarification techniques (see Chapter 3). Through group training exercises each committee was encouraged to brainstorm issues, seek clarification from others, and then work to reduce or identify the important issues to be tackled. There was to be no voting in any group, as voting tends to create winners and losers in a small group process. Thus, each person was asked to make a commitment to support group decisions through dialogue and debate. On the whole, the committees were very productive with this process as measured by the quantity, quality, and level of genuine commitment to their recommendations.

Lastly, it was decided that each task force would start and complete its work in six to eight weeks. A commitment was gained from each committee member to work for a short intensive period of time rather than stretching their work out over many months. There was a concern that a lengthy planning period would diffuse the energy of the committee members, and they would lose the focus of their intended task. This proved to be unfounded, as the Task Force on Computer Technology insisted on expanding their timetable to five months, mostly due to the earnestness of this group.

Building a Path for the Child Who Learns with Difficulty

The Pampa schools, typical of every community in America, have many children who neither learn when first presented material nor do they learn easily. Realizing that this is a major challenge for the public schools of Pampa, Texas, the At-Risk Task Force sought to build a path for student success through improved standards in parent involvement, school programs, policies and procedures, teacher, parent, and staff development, and community programs. A brief description of the quantity of work that was generated from the five at-risk committees is shown in Table 8.

The Committee on School Programs, for example, chose as its priorities the following areas: prejudice toward the slow learner, pupils who fall in the "cracks," sex education at the upper elementary level, improved access to vocational/academic programming, and reading in-

Table 8

Name of Committee	Number of Goals	Number of Objectives
Parent Involvement	7	7
School Programs	3	32
Policies and Procedures	4	6
Teacher, Parent , and Staff Development	4	14
Community Programs	5	20-25

struction at all levels. It is worthy to note that this committee, typical of so many others, wrote this statement as their vision for the year 2000:

> The thrust toward the future, through the process of Pampa 2000, involves a restructuring of the links between schools, the community, and the total environment. By addressing school programs, our task force proposes a future-focused curriculum in which educators and pupils create a bond between action and learning so that young people realize they are needed by society. Learning must be tied to the future so that it can give it structure and meaning. It is our belief that pupils need to know their own abilities, have a sense of their own importance, and know that they can succeed.

> To plan for 2000 the task force recommends careful academic placement of pupils through programs designed to identify early those who have developmental, emotional, and/or learning disabilities. A careful teaching system, based on a continuum of skills, will allow for accurate data in ascertaining what students know and do not know. More special counselors and specialized teachers must be assigned to children with "at-risk" status. All learning can be enhanced by early identification of disabilities, matching learning modes with teaching styles, and creating positive learning environments.

> Educational programming for 2000 demands flexibility. In the past, required courses and specific numbers of class/course offerings, while trying to achieve higher standards of learning, have actually resulted in rigid programming which leaves little room for creative teaching or learning. The community's concept of the Little Red Schoolhouse idea and the Self-Contained Classroom have to be broadened to include interaction between students and the community, more technological instruction and a wide vocational program. The year 2000 demands more than reading, writing and arithmetic. Pampa 2000 requires pupils who recognize their aptitudes, their place in our society, and their relationship to others.

This powerful vision for the Pampa schools served as a reminder that the significant planning of the PAMPA 2000 project would become more than a collection of words to be placed on a shelf, only to be dusted off when state accreditation teams visited the school district. The At-Risk Task Force did more than build lifeless plans; for example, they were bold in their recommendation to have a phone on each teacher's desk, to eliminate the tracking in middle school "remedial" classes, and to open summer school to hundreds of children needing additional time to satisfactorily complete their studies.

In addition, numerous parent volunteers have begun to walk the streets of Pampa in a newly established "Friendly Visitor" program. A group of parents from all parts of the community agree to be trained in effective intervention techniques with other parents. They then collect the names and addresses of children not coming to school and pay a friendly home visit asking parents if any assistance is needed in getting their child to come to school. The friendly visitor program has had a remarkable positive effect on many of the families with low-attending children.

These new program efforts have been highly successful for both the quality and quantity of results, but most importantly, because of the level of sincere commitment gained by each member on each task force committee. The notion that Pampa could graduate 100% of its students was born in the debate and consensus process of this task force – a birth that was eventually to give tremendous impetus to further restructuring the Pampa schools for improved student performance.

A Vision for Paving the Path with Technology

The quality of work conducted by the Task Force on Computer Technology was just as aggressive and thorough as the At-Risk Task Force. This Task Force was charged with developing a vision of what the schools should look like in the year 2000 in terms of technological support for classroom teachers and administrative staff. Thus, the Task Force was composed of four committees: elementary, middle school, high school, and administrative support computing. It operated in a very similar fashion to the At-Risk Task Force. Through committee assignments the task force met on a regular basis for several months, visited each Pampa school, reviewed recent literature and research, and visited other schools in California and in the Texas Panhandle and Dallas areas. Like the At-Risk Task Force, these committees worked to create a vision for the year 2000, to inventory and analyze existing technologies in the Pampa schools, and then to examine ways to close the gaps through recommended goals, objectives, and suggested first steps to the school board.

It was through this process that the Task Force concluded that the schools "are in the fourth quarter with no time outs, and we are behind" in preparing our children and teachers for the demands of a changing world. The Task Force further observed that the Pampa school district was deficient in many areas of technological assistance for teachers and students. In the strongest language the group reported that "the gaps in electronic technology that we have found ... cannot be tolerated in a school system striving for academic excellence." This is strong language to present to the school board, particularly when one considers that hundreds of citizens, teachers, and staff participated in constructing meaningful recommendations for improvement.

The Task Force on Computer Technology developed a brief but meaningful vision statement when it said

> Pampa school teachers are performing well, and Pampa students are being successful in many measurable ways. We recognize that our teachers deserve the best support that can be provided; we recognize that our mission is to succeed with every child; we recognize that continuous improvement is important to all professional educators—it is important to our children; it is important to our nation.

Based on an imperative to provide quality support to Pampa teachers, the Task Force identified mathematics as the key area for technological support in the classroom. In reviewing their report they chose mathematics because of the following reasons (keep in mind that Pampa class averages exceed national averages at every grade level).

- The majority of high school students do not qualify for high school algebra.
- Many of our best math students struggle with even the simplest math functions.
- In March 1989, 300 eighth grade students were tested for readiness to take high school algebra. Only forty satisfactorily demonstrated readiness—with the present twenty-seven eighth grade students in Algebra I, this represents only 21 percent of the total eighth grade.
- Approximately 20 percent of the eleventh grade students cannot meet minimum passing standards on the Texas state minimum competency test.
- Mathematics is highly sequential and CAI easily fits the educational program of each child in mathematics.

Based on this internal study and exhaustive research on the best use of technology, the Task Force made recommendations that will impact the teaching of mathematics in 175 classrooms for over 2,000 children in grades 1-9, as well as the writing skills of at least 500 high school students. Learning centers using computer technology also were installed at two high school sites to allow high school teachers the flexibility to individualize the instruction of low-achieving students in mathematics and other high school coursework. Further, recommendations from the Task Force included "Writing to Read" centers in six elementary schools, the expansion of video-disc technology to libraries, hook-up to satellite technology for teacher and staff training, and a relational student data base linking together counselors, principals, social workers, diagnosticians, and, ultimately, teachers for up-to-date information on the progress of any student.

Acceptance of these rather expensive but critical technologies was a considerable concern of the school board and other school leaders. It is true that the plans for this work were developed with extensive community involvement, but many citizens had not participated in the construction of these plans. Thus, parents and the larger civic clubs in town were all invited to visit and evaluate the quality of this technological effort. The reaction of each civic club to the school computer lab sites was overwhelmingly positive by citizens of all ages. Thus, the Pampa community is convinced that these technology-assisted plans will have a major and positive effect on the education programs of Pampa—and all because the Pampa community was mobilized to participate to create a vision through technology for a better educational future of thousands of Pampa children.

While the vision approach ultimately produced important results, the process did not have a sound footing against which all future action could be measured. The At-Risk and Computer Technology Task Forces were organized from the outside in and the bottom up. They were designed to create sensitivity to changing economic and environmental conditions. They served as a basis for generating a common understanding regarding better schools, and they were intended to provide renewed support to teachers, but they did not have a solid foundation insofar as the subject of continued school improvement was concerned. School and community leaders were concerned that the 1990 version of a "better schools vision" would become frozen and unadaptable to changing conditions at a future time. There was the real possibility that these plans would become similar to other plans: helpful at one point in time, but soon outdated and useless when circumstances, politics, personnel, and the economy would inevitably change again. Were these well-developed plans going to become a one-time event with little or no relationship to continued school improvement? In a second wave of planning, Pampa utilized the mission approach to strengthen the long-term commitment to outside-in and bottom-up school improvement.

Building the Path on Bedrock

"Values are the bedrock of any corporate culture" [4], and the mission approach to school planning begins with the identification of those core values or beliefs that define who we are and what we believe. As we experience the close of the American 20th century, public education is continuing to experience a confusion over what is valued about students, teachers, and learning. In previous generations it was clear that school was for the intellectual few, as homework was abundant and standards were rigorous. As Albert Shanker states,

> Times were simpler. Broken families were unusual unless a parent had died. Parents pushed their children to excel; mothers stayed home; commercial television didn't exist; drugs were practically unknown. Most students were respectful toward their teachers—their parents encouraged them in that—and school violence was rare. [5]

While these values persist, they no longer dominate our American culture.

Bill Cook [6] describes the shifting of values—the way we see ourselves and others, the role of family and government, our psychological and world view—as a natural process that is consistent with changing economic times. In the agrarian era the typical mother and father worked alongside each other, both sharing in income production and child-rearing. Later, the industrial age came to be characterized by assembly line work, standardization, and rigidity of social mores. This was the era when materialism came to dominate American values, but it also was the era of work for the sake of work. For the first time in history the father left home to become the sole income earner, and mothers were left alone to raise the children.

The more recent information age can be described as the period of "permanent impermanence." The globalization of information, the opening of competitive world markets, and the constant doubling of information in every professional field have resulted in a decline of American preeminence, resulting in an explosion of contrasting values in the larger American culture. In this era, both mother and father left home to work, and child-rearing became a shared responsibility with day-care schools, other "baby-sitters," and public schools.

This state of fluidity or impermanence has contributed to an acceptance that "less is more," or that the future could be worse than the present—as is evidenced by the conspicuous consumption and empty savings accounts of the 1960s, 1970s and 1980s.

With dramatic political and economic events in Europe and Asia as examples of rapid change, we are experiencing the sense that, as Drucker says,

> Values of people are no longer business values; they are professional values. Most people are no longer part of the business society; they are part of the knowledge society. If you go back to when your father was born and mine, knowledge was an ornament, a luxury – and now it is the very center. We worry if the kids don't do as well in math tests as others. No earlier civilization would have dreamed of paying any attention to something like this. The greatest changes in our society are going to be in education. [7]

If public school organizations have not escaped these swirling cultural changes, and if public school classrooms are constantly bombarded with the effects of family violence, drugs, alcohol, teenage pregnancy, and school programs that are mismatched with the changing service economy—while expectations for quality schooling continue to rise!—then is it not time for communities to identify and unite over what they believe about schools? Are teachers, administrators, and school boards clear about their values toward children and parents? Are public school organizations operating from a core set of values that are both well understood and articulated by everyone associated with the schools?

Peters and Waterman [8] emphasize that the sharing of common bedrock values is one of the key tenets of all successful organizations. They describe how the most successful organizations spend enormous energy on continuously clarifying and maintaining their sense of who they are and why they exist. Tom Watson, the founder of IBM, wrote, "Consider any great organization—one that has lasted over the years—I think you will find that it owes its resiliency not to its form of organization or administrative skills, but to the power of what we call beliefs and the appeal these beliefs have for its people." Watson further explains that effective and lasting organizations have to be prepared to change everything except the core values that drive the organization. If the organization will identify its beliefs and work to explain and protect those beliefs, then changes or improvements in service or product will come more naturally to the organization.

In the fall of 1988, the Pampa school district entered the second stage of planning from the bottom up and outside in. Fortified with seven days of intensive training in "strategic planning" by Dr. Bill

Cook, one school board member and two key administrators returned to Pampa with a sense of how to begin the process of bringing the community together, in order to identify the fundamental values that are important to learning and teaching in Pampa, Texas. With this effort a process was developed whereby individual members of the Pampa school organization could be held accountable for advancing and protecting the values of the organization to improve schooling for thousands of Pampa children. The Pampa school organization would now have a common set of beliefs that would eventually ignite the school district with an unprecedented amount of unity to continue the improvement of schooling for every child.

The strategic model is designed to improve targeted areas and is not intended to change everything that is in a school district. The planning is a step-by-step method (see Appendix E) that began with twenty-five citizens, representative of Pampa businesses, parents, and the school community. In an intensive retreat format, these individuals identified nine bedrock belief statements to guide and hold the Pampa school system accountable to. Two of the beliefs, for instance, include "every person has equal value and worth" and "the school, community, and family, through collaborative efforts, control the conditions for success." These beliefs have become the basis for guiding all future improvement efforts, as the school staff, school board and community can now ask, ". . . Is that practice consistent with our stated beliefs about individuals and teaching and learning in the Pampa schools?" In keeping with the power of these beliefs, the Pampa schools have begun the process of recognizing that there are certain commonly held values that cannot be violated—they are important enough to fight for—and that any school practice, skill, or organization is subject to change as circumstances, politics, and economic conditions vary with time. These beliefs are rudimentary; they are being institutionalized, and all practices can be measured against them.

The second step of the Strategic Planning Task Force was to construct a statement that identified the unique purpose—the reason for existence—of the Pampa school district. This statement was to become the *mission* of the Pampa schools and was designed to clarify for everyone the true purpose for working with children by teachers, parents, administrators, and the school board. The Pampa mission statement as designed by the Strategic Planning Task Force read as follows:

> The mission of Pampa ISD, the district in Texas committed to educational and operational excellence, is to graduate responsible, adaptable, creative

and successful citizens by providing a varied, innovative curriculum to all populations of students, taught in a nurturing, cooperative climate of mutual respect through the efficient utilization of family, school and community resources.

As Deal and Kennedy argue [9], the value of a commonly held set of beliefs is that people care about them. When they are well-articulated with a sense of unique mission, they manifest themselves in shared values as seen in the achievement of children, the performance of employees, in the advancement of careers, and in the articulation of goals in the school district. The combination of commonly accepted beliefs with a well-defined statement of purpose strengthens the teaching and administrative staff with the sustenance for continued improvement for every child in every school.

The third step of the Strategic Planning Task Force was to identify any strategic parameters that are expected of the Pampa organization. These parameters were designed to provide definition and clarity for decisions of all kinds at any level of the school organization. Parameters serve as guideposts, just as a fence line gives a garden or a large rolling wheat field definitions and character; they can limit or guide action toward decisions about teaching and learning. The Pampa group chose two strategic parameters that were to affect all future decisions:

- We will never allow failure to be final for any student.
- We will always base major program changes on current, accurate, and sufficient data to justify the changes.

These strategic parameters were designed to commit the Pampa school community to the success of all students and to direct school personnel toward the goal of being "data driven" in making all decisions. Armed with a set of commonly held beliefs, a statement of purpose, and two guideposts for directing future actions, the Pampa planning team was able to galvanize the entire school district of 500 employees and thousands of citizens into a growing success with every child.

The final step was to develop four organizational goals with matching action plans that would propel the Pampa school district toward greater teacher involvement, a sense of genuine efficacy on the part of all staff, and most importantly, accountability for better student results. The four major goals were to become the focus for redesigning many school practices, developing an intensive set of implementation activities, and revising job descriptions and job accountabilities for all administrators. The four goals were written in very quantifiable language for use within the school district, but also were written in more simplified language for display in all school and district offices, as well as for general distribution throughout the community. The goals were

- by 1990 to improve the self-esteem of all students by an average of 10 percent
- to graduate all entering high school freshmen in increasing increments of 80 percent by 1992, 90 percent by 1996 and 100 percent by the year 2000
- to have at least five National Merit Semi-Finalists or Finalists in each Senior Class by 1993
- beginning in 1995, to involve 95 percent of the high school graduates in post-secondary education or gainful employment

These goals are specific, but far-reaching, when one considers an annual high school dropout rate of 35 percent and the fact that there had not been a national merit scholar in the Pampa school district in over twelve years. Part of the strategic planning design was to develop strategies and then "action plans" that would deflect school activities into an improvement plan that would accomplish the four major goals.

The Strategic Planning Task Force identified eight strategies (see Appendix F) to carry out the four major goals. These strategies were eventually turned over to eight matching Action Plan Teams. These teams were charged with developing specific "action steps" for each of the strategies that eventually were to touch a host of programs in the K-12 grades. To gain acceptance, these eight bold strategies were systematically presented to administrators, campus leadership teams, faculty meetings, community civic clubs, and finally, at a district "celebration" event for the volunteer work of hundreds of employees in the Pampa school district.

At this event, the town Mayor and Chamber of Commerce President helped present certificates and different colored ribbons of appreciation to the many hundreds of volunteers in numerous school programs. A different colored ribbon was given to each staff member and teacher who volunteer extra time to the booster clubs, PTAs, speech, choir, band, athletic, handicapped, and vocational support groups. A few teachers volunteered their time to so many programs that they looked like Third World dictators under the weight of their many colored ribbons. At the conclusion of the celebration, teachers and other employees were asked to join an action team, but it was stressed that this was strictly voluntary. In fact, almost as an afterthought, sign-up tables were set up at the back of the auditorium. At the conclusion of the event, forty-two teachers went to the back of the auditorium and volunteered to join scores of other citizens on the eight action teams.

The plans developed by these action teams were wide-ranging and touched virtually every program in the Pampa school district. Like the work of the At-Risk and Computer Technology Task Forces, the Strategic Planning Task Force is currently in the process of implementing plans that significantly re-order the type and quality of work performed in the Pampa schools. The bottom-up and outside-in system of planning is difficult, time-consuming, and risky for any parties who have a vested interest in maintaining the status quo of school performance. While the mission approach to planning has given school personnel a clear mandate to continue to strive to achieve the four major district goals, it was the vision approach that managed to capture two pictures – the ideal and the present, with plans to close the gap – which proved extremely useful to advancing the work of the Pampa 2000 project. Coupled with improved standards for leadership, group performance, organization, the genuine involvement of teachers, parents, and businessmen, the Pampa school district has been projected into a future that is sure to bring greater school success to the next generation of Pampa children.

Troubleshooting

I've had community involvement before. It really did not amount to much. We met a couple of times, attendance was poor, and most of those who did attend regularly had an ax to grind. What did you do to get such impressive participation and outcomes from your task forces?

The issue of how to gain total organizational enthusiasm and commitment to improving school practices is a difficult one. The strength of any school district is the teachers. The Pampa schools had to give real planning power – the power to change things – to teachers and parents. The commitment to grow had to first come from each individual at the top of the organization, and the school board and superintendent had to be willing to devote the time and energy to planning. They constantly worked to flush out problems, to evaluate and reorganize some aspect of the total planning project. Second, they had to model positive attitudes, while insisting on honesty toward how children were performing. They trusted in the fact that teachers are actually the one group that really knows how Johnny and Susie are doing. School boards and administrators have to be sensitive to the strength of the school district, but also they have to be willing to take some of the heat for the existence of some of the conditions that create school failure. In addition, the school administrators have to be well trained in the complexities of successful planning efforts, and the project must be a top priority at all levels of the school organization. When school board members devote their time and energy to the total project, then it is easy to inspire other staff to believe that these efforts are worthwhile.

I'm not clear about your bottom-up and outside-in organization. Can you give me an example of how that works from your experience?

Specifically, you have to be willing to let teachers participate in making strategic decisions and allow other citizens (the non-experts) to participate at the operational level. For example, it is amazing how effective a teacher can be when it comes to making a multi-million dollar decision. This is true for any combination of issues, ranging from a change in computer systems to training programs. Similarly, parents and businessmen can be a lot more insightful about effective teaching practices, or classroom organizational issues, than educators are sometimes willing to admit. The trick is that you never know where expertise will emerge from, as it is not always from the person with the most credentials. At one very critical point in the debate over "every person has equal value and worth," a retired citizen in our community rose in opposition to the assertion that some children are better—better in academics, behavior, achievement—so they are not equal. This citizen declared that if the school system did not support the equal treatment of all children at all times, then she would lead a tax revolt against the school district. This brought great clarity to the Strategic Planning Task Force, and now everyone is held accountable to this important standard.

The Pampa 2000 project sounds very ambitious. I can see how it would galvanize a community behind its school district, but how did you get it started?

Again, honesty! No person actually wants children to do poorly or perform below their abilities. You have to be willing to learn the facts about how children are doing and then be dogged in pursuing answers to questions and problems. It has to begin with the dedication of the school board, the staff of administrators, and key teachers throughout the district. This means that you have to be willing to shed your authority for true dialogue, but you have to take personal responsibility for helping to design a school where all children can succeed. This is the first step, but it makes a tremendous difference if others are going to support you in your moments of doubt and confusion.

You have presented a seamless process for getting started in restructuring. Can you tell me about some of the problems you experienced and how you handled them?

Problems? We had plenty of problems. First, we did not always have the expertise to tackle certain jobs. Our administrators did not have many of the skills to internally manage the change process, nor did the top of the organization feel confident with promoting a process that really works. Thus, it was important to commit to training programs like Dr. Bill Cook's Strategic Planning and then to continuously relearn better methods for managing this change environment. Second, you have to be willing to pay the price of making personnel changes if key administrative staff members are unwilling – not reluctant, as that is normal – but absolutely unwilling to help open your system to teachers, parents, and businesses. Third, it always hurts when a teacher takes the change process very personally. You have to remember that teachers are the most underutilized work force in America, and it is imperative that you address this problem through the training of your committees and administrators. Fourth, you have to be willing to commit the necessary resources in your budget. Restructuring does not necessarily mean high expenses, but be prepared for this to happen and enlist your school board and community to help you solve this problem. If your school board and the leading teachers and citizens of the community are involved in making plans to reshape the programs of children, then you should have a group that is interested in seeing your schools improve.

Which do you recommend, the vision approach or the mission approach? What are the benefits and drawbacks of each?

They both work – if you pay careful attention to training the groups in teamwork and the consensus process, if you devote genuine support to each group, and if you are willing to accept suggestions for change. In terms of long-lasting sustainable change you should consider the advantages of the mission approach. With a vision approach you try to take two photographs of your system – one for the future and one for the present. This allows the process of change to be very deliberate, but what happens when three years later conditions and personnel change? The mission approach will be more time-consuming to the leadership and teachers of your organization, but it will commit your organization to a path of regenerating improvement from year-to-year. This approach is likely to be most rewarding to your teachers, staff, and administrators alike.

References

1. Peters, Thomas J. and Robert H. Waterman Jr. 1982. *In Search of Excellence*. New York, New York: Warner Communications Co., p. 212.
2. Bradford, David L., and Allan R. Cohen. 1984. *Managing for Excellence*. New York: John Wiley & Sons, p. 212.
3. Allstate Insurance Company. 1989. "Labor Force 2000: Corporate America Responds," Allstate Forum on Public Issues, p. 3.
4. Deal, Terrence E., and Allen A. Kennedy. 1982. *Corporate Cultures*. Reading, Massachusetts: Addision-Wesley Publishing, p. 21.
5. Shanker, Albert. 1990. "A Proposal for Using Incentives to Restructure our Public Schools," *Phi Delta Kappan* (January):346.
6. Cook, Bill. 1988. *Strategic Planning for America's Schools*. Arlington, Virginia: American Association of School Administrators, pp. 55-65.
7. Drucker, Peter. 1990. "Facing the 'Totally New and Dynamic,' " *Time* (January):6.
8. Peters and Waterman, op. cit., p. 280.
9. Deal and Kennedy, op. cit., pp. 25-30.

⑥ Getting Started in Restructuring— Alternative Scenarios

Chapter 5 has described how Pampa initiated restructuring. Other districts have pursued different approaches, but there are common features to those who have been most successful. Important to note here is that most of them did not say, in effect, "We ought to get started in restructuring because there is a lot of street talk about it, the board has been asking questions, and the union wants to know when we are going to treat teachers as professionals."

It is critical to get started in restructuring on the right basis, for powerful forces exist to prevent restructuring or impede its success. Restructuring calls for new roles for administrators, teachers, parents, and students. These groups may become frustrated, and subvert the intent of restructuring [1]. Tradition and fear may also combine to diminish the impact of restructuring. Power struggles can ensue as the old order is dismantled and a new one created [2]. The enthusiasm generated by a fresh concept may wane as problems arise that require increasing amounts of time and energy [3]. As formidable as these constraints are, however, some districts are experiencing a considerable amount of success. The following observations are drawn from seven successful districts[1] and two syntheses of research [4,5].

Creation of Need

All successful districts have begun by creating a need. This had the effect of coalescing all factions with an urgent desire for action to confront this need. Methods of doing this have been as divergent as the districts themselves. San Diego [6] formed a study group consisting of teachers, administrators, board members, parents, and com-

---

[1] San Diego, California; Lake Washington School District, #414, Kirkland, Washington; School district #12 in Adams County, Colorado; Dade County, Florida; Rochester, New York; Hammond, Indiana; Olton, Texas; Pampa, Texas.

munity representatives to study innovation and change. These study groups were followed by retreats with a more extended review of restructuring. Lake Washington [7] conducted surveys of teachers, parents, and students. The outcome of these surveys identified critical areas of need in the district. School District #12 in Adams County, Colorado [8], began with a review of the literature in a search for an appropriate response to the first wave of reform reports in the 1980s. In the case of School District #12, the reform reports served as the catalyst for change.

Dade County, Florida's [9] experience was quite different from that of the other districts studied. In the early 1970s, their board had approved several rules and regulations that shifted responsibility for certain budget decisions from the central office and area levels to individual schools. It was, however, another ten years before the board sensed that the community would support an enlargement of that beginning. The need in Dade County was not so much created as it was sensed by the board. Rochester, New York [10] did not create a need; rather, the need was surfaced by a community-wide initiative to improve the schools by the Urban League, an external agency. Need was created in Hammond, Indiana [11], by the precipitous decline in achievement at Hammond High, once one of the top high schools in the state.

Ray Kennison [12] reported that the Olton, Texas, district had been actively involved in a number of innovations during the 1970s – Right to Read, Pegasus Pace, and STAM. However, they became aware that these programs were not sufficient. Many of their lower-achieving students were simply not served and these isolated programs were having no influence on the school programs at large. The catalyst for their reform effort came from the local university, which emphasized the importance of a holistic approach to change, collaborative decision making, and sharing of power. A core group of Olton teachers and administrators began to educate the board and community about the need for change. The two syntheses of research found that a compelling case for restructuring tends to grow from acutely sensed need; need develops as awareness grows that the education system is not working and that what is needed is not mere tinkering, but a fundamental shift in assumptions [13].

Clarifying a Response

Identifying a need does not necessarily result in agreement on a response. Hord et al. [14] found that clarity on the specifics of the innovation is critical at the first stage of planning. Once the need was agreed upon in the districts included in this review, each proceeded in its own way to clarify a response. The retreats of the San Diego board members, administrators, and teacher association president culminated in the adoption of a policy statement and a set of belief statements on restructuring that committed them to long-term strategic planning to that end. Following their survey to determine needs, the Lake Washington professional staff adopted a mission statement and began work on a district master plan that would be reflected in building and teacher master plans. In constructing the master plan, the emphasis was on "relationships and interactions rather than rigid hierarchical structures or rules since people are more flexible than policies or procedures" [15].

School District #12 followed its review of the literature by evaluating four commercial models of school improvement. The I/D/E/A School Improvement Process was selected, and consultants from I/D/E/A led the clarification process of needs assessment and vision building. When the Dade County, Florida board sensed the community was ready for change, the school board approved a three-year pilot program in school-based management. The clarification process began subsequent to the approval as the board, administration, and teacher's union explored the issues that could arise with this new configuration. Out of this preliminary review, further clarification came with the adoption of four goals: to improve the educational program, to increase the focus of school system resources at the school level, to initiate shared decision making at the school level, and to increase community participation in the schools [16].

A further avenue for clarification was built in as all schools were invited to submit a proposal for participation in the pilot program. In the very process of fashioning the proposal, schools gained clarification as to how the process might work. Following the initiative of the Urban League, the parameters of the Rochester project became clarified in a wide-ranging contract negotiation with the teacher's union, in which permissive items such as professional issues as well as the mandatory items such as salary were openly considered. Management prerogatives as well as teacher accountability were discussed. The final contract was a transitional document—an agreement to agree, with details to be worked out later. Although this document was not exactly precise, it did provide an avenue for teachers to be directly involved in determining the specifics of restructuring, which was a clarifying activity.

Clarification in Hammond came as the result of grants from several public and private agencies and foundations to fund a two-year pilot project at the school. This project permitted the trial and testing of a number of avenues, and through this process clarity began to evolve. Clarity for Olton came as a result of a series of monthly meetings between the Olton core team of teachers and administrators and a local university team. Networking with three other school districts attending the meetings provided further clarity. The meetings centered on clarifying desired outcomes for students, developing a vision, and encouraging the change process. Olton followed up these meetings with their own meetings once a month to compare their current administrative/teaching practices with their desired student outcomes. Clarity about needed changes grew as these meetings progressed.

Syntheses of various research reports on restructuring note that clarification is a continuing requirement because restructuring represents not merely a reorganization of administrative responsibilities, but a fundamental change in the assumptions about what leaders do. The shift from planning and directing to consulting and collaborating requires ongoing vigilance and clarification [17,18]. Maintaining the conditions in which restructuring can succeed are as vital as creating the original conditions. Critical to this maintenance are a continuing dialogue with the union [19,20,21]; clarification of the balance of power and responsibilities between the central office and the school site [22]; definition of the balance of power at the school site between building administrators, teachers, parents, and students [23]; continued training and team building [24,25,26]; and continued focus on the original reasons for restructuring as difficulties, time constraints, and rivalries emerge [27].

The message from this review is that the process of creating conditions in which restructuring can be successful are as varied as the districts themselves. They can evolve over a period of years, as in Dade County, or spring up almost full grown, as in Rochester. They can result from interaction with an external agency, as in Olton, or from a reading of internal conditions, as in Lake Washington. They can develop as a result of study and deliberation, as in San Diego and District #12 in Adams County, or can evolve after a pilot project has been initiated, as in Hammond. Those who would create conditions in which restructuring can succeed must be attuned to their community and guide the energy already present. The diversity notwithstanding, however, the common denominator is that in some form or other all restructuring initiatives have drawn the different constituent groups together in study, dialogue, and collaboration. It is these same processes that sustain restructuring as ambiguities of role, confusions of structures, and uncertainties of relationships surface during implementation. The existence of commonalities makes it possible to develop a generic plan for implementation.

A Generic Plan for Implementation

Establishing the Need

Establishing the need once is usually not sufficient to build the commitment required for the sustained effort that will be necessary for restructuring. Therefore, the need should be confirmed by citing both internal data of student achievement and external sources of information about skills of local graduates such as that from colleges and businesses. The leader should not miss a chance to stress the need for change. As the problems begin to surface, members of the organization will begin to question the reasons for the changes. The reasons must be clear, confirmed, and convincing. Much of this should be accomplished in small study groups of teachers, administrators, parents, business persons, and community members at large. In communities where broad-based support has been attained, such as Pampa, the reasons should have been well-established, but even here it must be reiterated. If the needs can be phrased in a memorable fashion, such as "The A,B,C's for Change in Any Name School District," so much the better.

Establishing Beliefs

At times, the statement of beliefs might precede the identification of needs. At others, it will follow the identification of needs. But beliefs must be specifically stated. The reason that beliefs must be identified is that education is as much an emotional issue as a rational one. For example, the reasons for change might be quite logical and defensible, but if the grading policy or the discipline policy is altered to foster the change desired, it is a good bet that emotions will quickly surface. A consensus process must be followed in framing a statement of beliefs. In following a consensus process, a good rule to follow is that items of convenience must be decided in favor of the children; items of conviction must be dealt with [28].

If one is not careful, belief statements may be phrased in a way that preserves the status quo. There is good logic for this since the status quo often represents the only sense that most community members will have regarding how things should be. A useful guard against this is to appoint someone as a vigilante, whose responsibility is to guard against deference to the status quo.

The framing of belief statements can take a considerable amount of time and an emotional toll. There may well be times when the leader will be tempted to short-circuit the process and settle for a majority agreement. When so tempted, the leader must remember that he/she is building a basis for a long-term commitment to the changes and that commitment will fuel the energy, creativity, and persistence needed to make the changes successful. If the leader remains committed to achieving consensus, there are few beliefs that will not be agreed upon.

A sample statement of beliefs that has received acceptance by a number of districts is included in Appendix G. These beliefs are included not so that they might be duplicated and presented to another board, but as a frame of reference for administrators. It is most essential that each school district develop its own set of belief statements. Some may say that they don't want to reinvent the wheel by going through the sometimes arduous process of developing a set of belief statements. It may not be the wheel, however, that is important; it may be the process of invention [29]. This may be so because as groups go through the process of hammering out their beliefs, they also develop a deeper understanding of the action implications of those beliefs and a commitment to the behaviors required to make those beliefs a reality. As in the statement of need, if the beliefs can be phrased in a memorable manner, they are more likely to guide the decisions of the organizational members on a regular basis.

Inducing Change

Once the need for change has been established (establishing rational reasons for change) and a statement of beliefs has been developed (establishing an emotional commitment to change), change initiatives can proceed along several lines. The organizational leader may lead a policy analysis review to determine what policies currently in place are preventing needed actions from taking place and what policies are requiring actions that prevent the achievement of the beliefs or responsiveness to the needs. Suppose, for example, that there is a belief statement regarding the worth and dignity of every individual while at the same time there is a policy statement permitting paddling. To take another example, there might be a policy requiring the board to use local contractors; a belief statement might say that all students have a right to the best education the district can afford. If the effect of the board policy has been to purchase construction at a higher price or materials of poorer quality, the policy might have to be revised in light of the belief statement. See Appendix H for a process for analyzing board policy.

Additionally, a discrepancy analysis might be constructed. In this process, one might develop an instrument similar to the one in Appendix I, based on the district's particular statement of needs and beliefs. Once discrepancies have been established between "what is" and "what should be," district administrators and board members have clear mandates for action.

Yet another way to induce change is to provide a series of open-ended statements such as those in Appendix J. These statements will stimulate thinking about the current status and may identify needed changes in existing policies, practices, or habits. Most of the early changes will concern routine issues or cosmetic changes. These are necessary to establish the practices of collaboration and to develop the trust that is essential for the next phase of more substantive changes.

Substantive Change

Substantive change deals with the core issues of curriculum and instruction. As the essentials of curriculum and instruction were dealt with in Chapter 4, only the process will be addressed here. Often teachers may begin to consider curriculum and instructional matters in the process of dealing with the policy issues above. If that has not occurred, however, then the leader needs to start the process of examining critical issues in curriculum and instruction.

There are several ways the leader may proceed in order to foster attention to these issues. Taking the belief statements one by one, the leader may ask teachers to contrast current practices in curriculum/instruction with the implications of these statements. The leader may distribute articles on emergent research concerning human cognition, curriculum, or instruction and then lead a discussion (or better yet, ask a teacher-leader to chair a discussion) on the implications for current practice. The leader might bring a speaker to the district or send a team of teachers to a district or a conference, which can stimulate a contrast between prevailing practices and improved practice. Peer observations of one another's teaching can cause an examination of current practice. Criticism of the teacher observed must be avoided; rather, seeking best practice must be the focus.

Care must be taken that any changes introduced conform with the needs and the beliefs statements. One possible result of sending teachers to other districts or conferences is that they could hear a charismatic speaker and become captivated by the person, instead of considering the substance of the concept in light of the commitments of the district. This must be avoided. Any changes in district programs should grow out of the perceived needs of the district and should become part of a holistic plan, not imposed as an add-on. Primarily, then, these outside sources will be for stimulation and perhaps adaptation rather than adoption. During this time, the administrator should be watchful for the predictable stages of the change process.

Stages in the Change Process

Typically, change will go through several stages. The following stages are likely to be experienced in one fashion or another.

Planning and Initiation

In this stage the beliefs have been well-established and the group has moved on to the consideration of concrete actions that will meet the expectations of those beliefs. Care must be exercised here that the group does not simply adopt a canned program. Adopting a canned program permits the group members to remove themselves from the investment required when the program is developed locally. Not only is the investment missing, but so is the tailoring of the program to meet local needs. If a charismatic individual has introduced the program, the initial enthusiasm might be quite high, but lacking the personal investment required of a locally developed response, effort and commitment may wane rather quickly. At its best, this stage represents the clarification of goals, the relation of the goals to local needs and beliefs, and the identification of material and human resources that can aid in the change. First steps are planned and responsibilities are assigned/accepted.

Momentum

In this stage, goal-directed activities begin to accelerate. Teachers and administrators begin to see how they fit in; initial efforts may be noted and appreciated by students, parents, and administrators, and feelings of personal worth may grow.

Problems

As the change efforts continue, problems will develop. Varying interpretations of the goals may surface, responsibilities and meetings may multiply, traditional habits and practices may have to give way to the new with resultant feelings of anxiety, the goals may seem increasingly improbable/impossible to attain, and the weaknesses or reluctance of some participants may surface. It is at this point that the administrator may have to confront his own commitment to the changes. Assuming that the changes are holistic in nature (not just adopting a new writing program or hooking students up to computers, but part of an overall strategy of changing the educational system to prepare students for the 21st century), the administrator will need to provide support and encouragement while at the same time reminding the teachers of the overall goals of the changes and providing help to those experiencing difficulty (perhaps through peer-assistance arrangements).

Turning Point

At this point the problems continue to mount or have been dealt with in such a way that the change initiatives proceed. Complaints will likely be of one or two types—doubts about one's own ability to make the changes or doubts that the changes will be worth the effort. The administrator must recognize the source of the doubts and move quickly to resolve them. Trust in others and confidence in the ability of one's subordinates (even perhaps when they have not always acted in a responsible manner) is very important at this stage. One reason they may not have acted responsibly in the past may have been the organizational disincentives of the bureaucratic system. If modifications of the change are in order (as they may well be), the leader must take care that the modifications do not move the organization backwards toward reinstitutionalizing bureaucratic practices.

Institutionalization or Termination

If the administrator has moved quickly to solve mechanical problems such as supplies, availability of resources, or assistance for those needing help, over time the culture of the organization can change and the changes can become institutionalized. This might take from three to five years. If on the other hand discontent is permitted to grow and little help or assistance is provided from the leadership, then the changes will at best be given lip-service. At worst, the failed change effort may make other changes difficult or impossible for some time.

Districtwide Change or School-by-School?

A decision that must be made at an early stage is whether the changes should be mounted on a districtwide basis or if each school should be encouraged to develop a flavor of its own. Those who favor choice and competition between schools would tend to favor the latter. Those who seek a uniform level of quality might tend to favor the former. There are potential advantages and disadvantages to either approach. The uniform approach would give a sense of a standard level of quality to parents and the public, would permit ease of transfer from one school to another in a district, would permit economies of scale in the purchase of materials and so forth, and would permit transfer of teachers from one building to another, to name a few advantages.

On the negative side, it might well reintroduce the scientific management approach to planning (that is, find the best way, train everyone in the best way, monitor for compliance, and provide remediation), might rob teachers and buildings of initiative, might fail to serve the needs of a subcommunity within a school district, and could reduce the amount of accountability (if a uniform process is required, then it is the process that is accountable, not individual buildings or teachers). The negatives of a school-by-school approach are largely the positives of a districtwide approach, and vice versa.

In order to deal with this dilemma, the school leader might be reminded of the loose-tight approach to school leadership. There can be parameters and accountability expectations that apply to all schools, while still leaving the opportunity for individual schools to work out their unique responses. This loose-tight approach provides for some uniformity of expectations and accountability, with sufficient opportunity for individual buildings and teachers to exercise initiative. Guidance for accountability measures and parameters may be gained from the Chapter 4 discussion of authentic assessment. A plan for phasing in school restructuring on a school-by-school basis is presented in Appendix K.

Organizing for Continuous Change

Toffler has noted that organizations of the future will be constantly reshaping themselves as the pace of change accelerates and organizations have to change in order to remain competitive. Whether the whole district or school-by-school approach to change is taken, there will need to be both a school-level improvement committee and a district-level committee. In a large district there may have to be subdistrict improvement committees. The committee should be composed of parents, teachers, and administrators (and perhaps a business person and a student). Election should be by the various constituent groups. The school-level groups should elect a representative from each constituency to the subdistrict or district group. The purpose of these groups would be both to review the progress of the school toward meeting its objectives and to propose new responses to emergent needs.

Board policy should define the status of these groups, specifying their areas of authority and the limits of their authority. Some possible areas of authority include establishing goals based on school-wide assessments of needs, developing or choosing curricula, determining instructional methods, providing training for parents, working in concert with other district schools to align curricula, allocating school funds based on goals and needs, determining numbers of staff and positions needed, and hiring staff [30]. It is recommended that the board specify the areas in which the school committee has authority to make decisions, areas in which the school committee may only make recommendations to the board, and conditions under which the board will be willing to alter district practices for a particular school committee [31].

Changing Roles in the Restructured Organization

As increasing authority for decision making is moved to the school site, the roles of district personnel must shift. The superintendent must constantly monitor the system for regression to bureaucratic practices; act as an advocate for restructuring; support and encourage restructuring practices; display trust in and support for teachers, administrators, and parents as they practice their responsibilities; and support schools and the school committees when the troubles develop. A key role for the superintendent is to prepare the board for restructuring and keep them informed as restructuring develops. Board members must not expect results too quickly and must be prepared for a certain amount of ambiguity as the process develops.

Central office personnel must shift from advocating a particular change and installing state-mandated practices to assisting school committees in their own change practices. It is largely up to the superintendent to ensure that central office personnel make this change in practice from installing and monitoring for compliance to assisting school-initiated changes. The principal has one of the most critical roles, for it is largely up to him/her to model the change practices, to install them, and to learn to lead groups in collaborative decision making on a consensus basis. It is also the job of the principal to form and operate the school committees and to resist engaging in bureaucratic leadership practices when teachers, parents, and others may expect him to do so and may even be critical at the slow pace dictated by consensus decision making.

Teachers must accept a much larger role in decision making than before. While to a degree this will be welcomed by teachers, they may well grate under the requirements of more meetings, the need to hear everyone out, the blind alleys that may be pursued, and so forth. Both teachers and principals may experience anxiety at the enlarged role of parents in decision making. For their part, the parents will have to learn to speak for parents as a group rather than pursuing selfish agendas. They will have to refrain from impatience when school personnel struggle with a decision that may seem obvious to the parents, avoid criticizing particular teachers, and keep the school committee focused on service to the student.

Students as well must serve as a barometer for the committee. As such, they can inform the committee of how close to the mark the decisions of the committee are coming, can serve as liaisons to the rest of the students, can take student concerns to the committee, and so forth. Businesspersons should refrain from attempting to tell the rest of the committee members how things ought to be done and should also refrain from drawing comparisons too directly between private business practices and those of the public school. On the positive side, businesspersons can keep the committee alert to the needs of business, emergent practices in business, and the skills and qualities that graduates both possess and lack.

Decision Screen

A key point of confusion can be the question of which decisions should be made at which levels. In general, decisions should be made at the lowest level possible in the organization. It might be good to determine whether the best interests of the children require a district-wide policy. If not, then site-based practices should be encouraged. A good test always is to ask if the policy is being made at the district level merely out of tradition or habit. Even if one suggests that the law requires a district policy, it is always good to ask for the specific law (sometimes there isn't one). Another good guide is to determine whether the policy is absolutely required at the district level; often-times it develops that a school-level policy might not only be permissible, but might save the board a great deal of stress. As restructuring is being implemented, there will be a strong tendency to continue making most decisions at the district level. Applying a decision screen such as this one can break such a tradition.

Summary

Districts have created the need for change in a variety of ways. Prevailingly they have built upon factors already present in the district or concerns already felt. Administrators who would introduce restructuring into the district are well advised to be sensitive to the windows of opportunity through which they can move. Once the need is identified, administrators must surface and give visibility to the beliefs that form the core commitments of the district. The beliefs have a better chance of influencing practice on a daily basis if they are concise and phrased in some catchy or memorable manner. While change might be initiated in organizational structures and relationships, substantive change in the key areas of curriculum and instruction should be the ultimate target of restructuring.

Change initiatives usually move through identifiable stages: (1) planning and initiation, (2) momentum, (3) problems, (4) the turning point, and (5) institutionalization. There are several points at which the change process can falter, and it is important that the leader be prepared to supply needed encouragement/support at those times. The issue of whether change should occur at the district level or at the school level was discussed. Strengths and problems are apparent in either approach. Perhaps the best resolution is to have district-level expectations and parameters while simultaneously giving schools wide latitude to plan instructional and curricular responses. Role confusion and confusion about which decisions should be made at which levels can result when the major changes required by restructuring are implemented. Careful delineation of the new roles, together with vigilance on the part of school leaders, can minimize role confusion. Use of a decision screen can help administrators to assert the primacy of decision making at the school level and to resist the bureaucratic tendency to push (or pull!) decision making up to the district level.

Troubleshooting

You have made the point about introducing restructuring by building on factors or concerns that already exist in the district. Most of the factors in my district are constituent-oriented—unions are looking out for the teachers, parents of special education students are pressing me for additional services that are expensive, community members press me for lower taxes, and so forth. Is there something I am missing?

I expect those same forces exist in every district in the country.

There seem to be more forces pulling districts apart than there are pulling them together. The key obviously is to find or create some need that will help all the advocacy groups shift their attention from their own narrow interests to those of the larger good as a whole. Remember that while some of the districts did build on concerns that evolved in the natural order of change, some of the districts structured study groups, retreats, or surveys and those provided the impetus for restructuring. Perhaps the best you can do is to survey what is going on presently in the district, and see if one of the following questions might provide the focus for starting in restructuring.

- Is the district considering a change in grade levels, perhaps moving from a junior high structure to a middle school structure?
- Is some collaboration with a college or university brewing? For example, are you considering starting a Professional Development School such as the one envisioned by the Holmes Group?
- Are you considering a major investment in technology?
- Is the district anticipating a major curriculum revision?
- Have there been budgetary changes that will require a review of all programs?

The point is that rather than approaching these as isolated issues and dealing with them on an ad hoc or piecemeal basis, you can use these issues as springboards to consider the fundamental beliefs of the members of the school community and use these belief statements as the basis for conducting a discrepancy analysis. This discrepancy analysis will provide you with a mandate for substantial change. The issues you mention about the union's concern for increased teacher pay or the community's desire for lower taxes can be enlarged to review the functions and purposes of the school. If the community comes to believe that the schools should prepare children for life in the 21st century, and helps shape what that school should look like, they are likely to be much more willing to pay taxes for support of that school.

How do I know that if I open things up the way your response suggests, I won't open up a Pandora's Box? The public might express a lot of expectations far in excess of our ability to deliver or their willingness to pay.

If your district has had a history of being closed (practicing control of information, accepting little input, etc.), there may well be some pent-up frustrations, suspicions, and outright hostility. Your best response is to stay steady on course, acknowledge past wrongs and express a willingness to deal with them, and keep focusing on the target – students prepared for success in the 21st century. Remember, when you open your district up, you are not creating the hostility, frustration, and suspicion, you are simply providing an avenue for its expression. You may be sure that the concerns that surface have operated to diminish the effectiveness of your program. While a smooth-sailing ship may be comforting to the captain, a ship in which concerns can be openly expressed and dealt with is probably a healthier ship (and certainly a healthier organization).

I thought one of the key elements of restructuring was school-based management. Yet, you raise the question of whether change should be at the district or the school level. Can you clarify?

I can see how this was confusing for you. Some school districts, Pampa for example, have used a series of representative committees, elected from each school, to make the general decisions. Then each school, also through a representative committee, plans implementation of the district-level decisions. The result is a uniform curriculum implemented with variations on the individual campuses. By contrast, Santa Fe school district has a number of unique school programs that offer various options to parents. Teachers in each of these districts tell of their increased participation in critical school matters and of their renewed commitment as a result.

Implementation Checklist

_____ 1. A clear and compelling need has been established.

_____ 2. The need has grown from a concern deeply embedded in the district itself.

_____ 3. The need is recognized by a large majority of school personnel and the community at large.

_____ 4. The need is sufficiently broad that it requires a holistic response rather than a mere change in the program or in the organizational chart.

_____ 5. A belief statement, growing out of or compatible with the need, has been fashioned by a broad constituency.

_____ 6. A number of task forces with representatives from both the schools and the community have been organized to make recommendations to the board for changes in school programs based on the needs and beliefs.

_____ 7. School personnel are fully aware of the stages that the change process goes through.

_____ 8. School personnel have been warned not to be fooled by the momentum stage of the change process into thinking that the change will be painless.

_____ 9. School personnel have been provided with specific suggestions for action when the problems stage of the change process develops.

_____ 10. School personnel have experienced role play and other reality-based opportunities to practice for their changed roles.

_____ 11. A decision screen has been developed.

_____ 12. School leaders are familiar with the use of the decision screen to assure that as many decisions as possible are made at the school level.

_____ 13. School leaders use the decision screen to guard against moving the decision-making process back up the organizational chart.

References

1. Decker, E. 1977. *Site Management: An Analysis of the Concepts and Fundamental Operational Components Associated with the Delegation of Decision-Making Authority and Control of Resources to the School-Site Level in the California Public School System.* Sacramento, CA: California State Department of Education.

2. White, P. 1989. "An Overview of School-based Management: What Does the Research Say?" *NASSP Bulletin*, 73:1-8.

3. Harris, B. 1975. *Supervisory Behavior in Education.* Englewood Cliffs, NJ: Prentice-Hall.

4. David, J. 1989. "Synthesis of Research on School-based Management," *Educational Leadership*, 46:45-53.

5. White, P. loc. cit.

6. Payzant, T. 1989. "To Restructure School, We've Changed the Way the Bureaucracy Works," *American School Board Journal*, 176:19-20.

7. Scarr, L. 1988. "Lake Washington's Master Plan—A System for Growth," *Educational Leadership*, 46:13-16.

8. Harrison, C., J. Killion, and J. Mitchell. 1989. "Site-based Management: The Realities of Implementation," *Educational Leadership*, 46:55-58.

9. Gomez, J. 1989. "The Path to School-based Management Isn't Smooth, but We're Scaling the Obstacles One by One," *American School Board Journal*, 176: 20-22.

10. Urbanski, A. 1988. "The Rochester Contract: A Status Report", Educational Leadership, 46:13-16.

11. Casner-Lotto, J. 1988. "Expanding the Teacher's Role: Hammond's School Improvement Process," *Educational Leadership*, 45:349-353.

12. Kennison, R. Personal communication with the superintendent of the Olton, ISD schools (October 6, 1989).

13. David, J. loc. cit.

14. Hord, S., W. Rutherford, L. Huling-Austin, and G. Hall. 1987. *Taking Charge of Change*. Alexandria, VA: The Association for Supervision and Curriculum Development.

15. Scarr, L. loc. cit.

16. Gomez, J. loc. cit.

17. David, J. loc. cit.

18. White, P. loc. cit.

19. Casner-Lotto, J. loc. cit.

20. Gomez, J. loc. cit.

21. Urbanski, A. loc. cit.

22. Brooke, M. 1984. *Centralization and Autonomy; A Study in Organizational Behavior*. London: Holt, Rinehart, and Winston.

23. White, P. loc. cit.

24. Griffith, H. Personal communication (September 14, 1989).

25. Kennison, R. loc. cit.

26. White, P. loc. cit.

27. Gomez, J. loc. cit.

28. Moses, M. 1990. *The Peak Performance School*. Westbury, NY: J. L. Wilkerson Publishing Co.

29. McLaughlin, M. 1976. "Implementation as Mutual Adaptation: Change in Classroom Organization," Teacher's College Record, 77(3):339-351.

30. Hansen, B. and C. Marburger. 1989. *School Based Improvement*. Columbia, MD: The National Committee for Citizens in Education.

31. Ibid.

7 Fostering Restructuring—
Orientation and Maintenance

A brief discussion of open and closed systems will help establish the background for the treatment of issues in this chapter. Closed systems are systems that are relatively immune from external influence. If such a system is also characterized by a dominant (e.g., top-down) authority structure, then the induction of change becomes a simple straight-line process. One devises the change from the top, specifies the role of the subparts of the system, and initiates the change—a relatively simple approach to change. Mechanical devices are good examples of strictly closed systems; a desired change in the output of the device can be produced by changing the parts of the device itself. On the negative side, closed systems tend toward entropy, a term from thermodynamics meaning, in effect, that closed systems will eventually reach a state in which there is no organization. Bureaucracies, the organizational equivalent of closed systems, can reach a state of chaos; that is, they no longer serve the purpose for which they were originally intended.

Open systems, by contrast, are subject to influence by the external environment. If they are also characterized by an organic (upward and lateral as well as downward) hierarchy, then initiation of change becomes a very complex process. This is true because any attempt at change is subject to innumerable potential influences from outside, as well as inside, the organization. On the other hand, since the system is open, entropy does not pose a problem. Since most public organizations are subject to innumerable external as well as internal influences, they tend to resemble open systems more nearly than closed ones. Dominant hierarchies tend to be found in closed systems, whereas organic hierarchies tend to be found in open systems. This is true because open systems simply do not allow for the control necessary for dominant hierarchies to flourish.

While change is relatively simple to induce in closed, dominant hierarchies, it is much more complex in open, organic, hierarchical systems. In a closed system, if one can control the main cog and give it a spin, then all the other cogs will move accordingly. In an open system, one may not be able to identify the main cog, or it may shift from case to case, or it may even shift from the time the change initiative starts until it is complete. Because education systems tend to be more open and organic, change must be approached in a holistic fashion, giving attention to numerous factors that may impinge on the change (and which the change itself might affect). The induction of change is at the heart of restructuring. David Kearns, for example, has stated that education does not need to be "improved" or modified; rather, the fundamental concepts upon which it is based need to be restructured.

Orientation

Overarching Goals and Symbols

In an open system, goals and symbols become vital in channeling all efforts in the direction that the organization has committed itself to. Overarching goals guide the work of the members in the organization on a day-to-day basis. Such goals must be cogent and yet have meaning for those in the organization. Below is a sample list of slogans for districts that are typical of many school districts.

(1) Expect Success
(2) Excellence in Education
(3) Where Quality Education Is a Fact
(4) Leading the Way
(5) Growing in Excellence
(6) Accent on Education
(7) Shaping the Future through Our Schools

While there is a certain amount of optimism in the slogans above, they may not provide the needed focus in an open organization. For example, #3 suggests that the school district has already arrived at its goals, #6 represents a mild endorsement of the main purpose of schools, and #7 certainly states a fact without any hint of what that future might be. Statements #1, #2, and #4 are just too general to provide the necessary guidance to action. By contrast, the Pampa slogan was, "Success for one; success for all." This logo captures their commitment to the education of all children—a central thrust in Pampa.

On a more detailed basis, here are the corporate creeds of some successful international corporations:

(1) Nissan Motor Co. – "The enrichment of society through commitment to customer satisfaction"
(2) Honda Motor Co. – "Responding to global customers' demands by manufacturing products of high performance and low cost"
(3) Toyota Motor Corp. – "To contribute actively to the economic and social development of Japan and the world by maintaining a constant devotion to good products and good ideas"
(4) Toshiba Corp. – "To contribute to the progress and development of society by working to forge a rich and healthful environment for people to live in, creating new value on the basis of respect for the human being"
(5) NEC Corp. – "Helping people lead richer, more human lives by using the convenient functions of various systems born of the union of computers and communications"

Note in each of these statements the emphasis on the betterment of humanity and society through the business of the company. The emphasis of the Pampa district on success for all carries this same message for both the employees of the district and their clients (students and parents).

Symbols play an equally important part in the orientation of school employees. In one school district, for example, the school board had met on a raised platform, looking down on the employees and citizens of the district. On the arrival of the new superintendent, one of his first acts was to remove the platform and replace it with a table so all were on the same level. Another act was to abolish all reserved parking places. These had formerly been reserved for the administrators at the central office, leaving the clerical staff to scramble for spaces wherever they could. Another act was to establish a prestigious committee to examine minority recruiting and hiring practices in the district. Each of these symbolic acts was intended to convey the message that equity is very important in this district. Other symbolic acts can include issues that get placed on agendas, who gets to speak and for how long, who gets invited to meetings, what is acted on and what postponed, and so forth. Attention to an overarching goal statement and symbols/symbolic acts is critical in the orientation phase.

Building the Flexible/Responsive Organization

One of the critical acts in orientation is to change the operating assumptions of the members of the organization. They will have adopted behaviors that have paid off for them over a period of years, and it will be necessary to take definitive action in order to reshape those behaviors. The restructured school organization must recognize six critical operational premises:

(1) The structure should be designed around organizational purposes (e.g., to facilitate the growth/development of individuals who are our clients and our employees).
(2) The superintendent has centralized authority/responsibility.
(3) Decentralization into attendance units (schools) should be accompanied by reasonable operational autonomy.
(4) Work of the superintendency should derive in part from the fact that schools cannot be completely self-sufficient.
(5) Levels of authority should be kept to a minimum (a flat organization).
(6) Each individual in the organization should be accountable to one superior; accountability of higher authority for acts of its subordinate should be absolute.

With the above common understandings, the superintendent's staff can be asked to participate in framing a definition of their philosophical and organizational "reason to be." Once this is accomplished, they can then be asked to review and reconcile that statement with the district mission, objectives, and parameters as well as with the principles of participative management. With these understandings, the central office staff can then be asked to address the following process issues.

- *Mission and roles*—Reason for your existence in relation to the mission of the organization. For example, what are your commitments; who do you serve?
- *Key results areas*—Where are your time, energy, and talent put? For example, do you use time for strategic planning, staff development, curriculum revision, or purchasing?
- *Indicators*—What will be the measurement of the level of achievement of your results areas? For example, what is the effectiveness of documents produced, the success of consulting, the efficiency of purchasing, etc.?
- *Objectives*—These are statements of measurable results.
- *Action Steps*—What program steps, schedule, budget, accountability review, and adjustments can you provide?
- *Controls*—What deadlines, review and progress reports, and formative and summative evaluations exist?

Using this process model will assist the ability of the central office staff to view their new role as advocates for teachers and students. Such an approach to building a responsive organization stands in sharp contrast to the job description process detailed below (a process followed by a major school consulting group) which appears to view educational organizations as closed entities.

- Initial job performance statements are drafted by the central agency.
- Initial drafts are reviewed by a small group of exemplary practitioners.
- Samples of representative practitioners are identified for each position.
- Job performance statements are sent out to the groups of practitioners.
- Based on feedback, job statements are revised and returned to the group of practitioners.
- Final revisions are made by central staff.

Such a process will predictably produce a generic job description that reinforces conventional practice, rather than a job description that fosters a more responsive, entrepreneurial organization.

Action Planning

Action planning is another phase of the process of orienting the members of the organization to their changed roles. The purpose of action planning is to engage those who will carry out the plans in the construction of the plan. In a small district, action planning might be carried out by the superintendent and his staff on a school-by-school basis. In larger districts where this would be impractical, the superintendent and his staff will hold a series of meetings with the building principals, working them through the action planning process; then the principals will return to their buildings and conduct the process with their staffs. If this latter process is followed, the building principals must be reminded throughout the day of activities that they will be expected to replicate this process with their staffs.

In view of this expectation, time must be provided for participants to practice the behaviors they are to implement. The day should begin with a renewal of team-building and consensus-building exercises as described in Chapter 3. The schedule of a typical action planning meeting held with the Pampa high school administrators, counselors, and teacher representatives is shown in Table 9.

For additional clarification, the activities in the agenda will be discussed further. The 8:45 item, "Let's get acquainted," consisted of persons in the group telling something about their personal backgrounds. Some were divorced, some were from poor families, some had

TABLE 9

Leadership Team Retreat
Pampa High School
November 14, 1987

Objectives:

   To introduce consensus as a tool for decision making

   To begin team-building

   To draw upon the resources of the group to build an action plan for Pampa High School

8:30	Introduction
8:45	Team-building: Let's get acquainted
9:40	Characteristics I value in a colleague—consensus building
10:30	Break
10:45	Building the agenda
	• Feedback
	• Opportunities
	• Process model for today's activities
11:05	Building an action plan item I
	• Teachers
	• Counselors
	• Administrators
12:15	Lunch
12:45	Groups report from morning work—20 minutes per group
1:45	Sharing successful changes
2:15	Break
2:30	Building an action plan item II
3:30	Group reports
4:30	Feedback/evaluation
4:45	Conclusions
5:05	Closure: one hope I have for Pampa High School

never known their fathers or came from broken households, some had been the teacher's pet in school. Each told something personal about his/her life history, a school experience, and an adult life experience. Even though these people had worked together for as long as twenty years, they learned things about each other in this exercise that they had never known before. The effect of this exercise was to draw the group closer together, to learn of each other's motives, drives, and ambitions, thus beginning the process of team-building.

The 9:40 exercise, "Characteristics I value in a colleague," had a twofold purpose. One was to practice the skills of consensus-building (see Chapter 3); the other was to uncover qualities this group valued in a colleague. These qualities were absorbed by the other group members and subtly became the model for their own group behavior. This exercise may be carried out in two steps. In the first step, the groups (no group should be larger than six members) may brainstorm characteristics they value in a group member. These items from the small groups may be combined into a master list. Then from this master list the small groups can be asked to pick the three they value the most and the three they value the least, using the consensus-building process described in Chapter 3. Each small group then reports back to the whole group and a master list of the most and least desired group member characteristics is developed.

An alternative to this process is to present the small groups with a list of group characteristics, thus eliminating the brainstorming step. This has the advantage of speeding up the exercise. Sample characteristics might be "Listens attentively," "Asks for details," "Refrains from disagreeing," "Points out applicable rules or policies," and "Expresses frustration when appropriate." A list of twelve or fifteen would be sufficient.

The 10:45 exercise, "Building the agenda," and the 11:05 exercise, "Building an action plan," refer to developing a process for insuring the long-term success of the students, teachers, counselors, administrators, and staff. Participants can be asked to agree on what they feel are the most significant problems (or opportunities) at their school. The action planning begins when they are then asked to brainstorm all potential solutions. Finally, they are asked to prioritize those solutions. For this exercise, small horizonal groups meet (e.g., teachers with teachers, counselors with counselors, etc.). The following were some of the problems (opportunities) developed by some of the groups at the Pampa meeting.

Teachers—Problems

- Courses offering placement policies, procedures, and practices need to improve.
- More attention must be paid to philosophy, caring, consistency, follow-through, and teaching all kids.
- Conflicts exist regarding state vs. local requirements, student attitudes about honors courses, etc.

Teachers—Solutions

- Identify best practices in other places.
- Have teachers evaluate their own efforts, policies, practices, etc.
- Identify educationally meaningful criteria for honors,

remedial, and other course placement. Involve teachers, counselors, administration, and parents in defining criteria.
- Emphasize development, not remediation.
- Define exemption policies.
- Define the how and who of homework.
- Improve quality of teaching and teacher attitudes.
- Build reinforcers for working with any and all students.
- Train to work with all students.

Administrators—Problems

- Information flow is insufficient.
- Interruptions are constant.
- There is no feedback on decisions.
- Input is lacking at all levels.
- Decision-making groups are not connected.
- Administrators and teachers are insecure in their roles.
- The flow of information is inconsistent.
- "Killer phrases" are detrimental.

Administrators—Solutions

- Involve teachers in administration-related problems, then hold everyone accountable.
- Write/complete a handbook to teacher/staff.
- Study paperwork flow and reduce.
- Brief in-service staff on their new roles.

The second action planning at 2:30 focused on participation/engagement. Participation/engagement referred to both the level and the quality of participation by students, teachers, counselors, administrators, and staff in all student activities. A high-quality school, they noted, is one that includes high quality involvement in student academic, co-curricular, and extracurricular programs. The leadership team was asked to build an action plan that would support improved participation by students and employees in the programs of the high school. The team was divided into three groups made up of a mixture of teachers, counselors, and administrators (a vertical team). After each of the small groups completed their action planning, they made a report of their recommendations to the large group. Some of their recommendations appear next.

Problem Manifestations

- Low number of participants
- Low level of audience support
- Lack of opportunities for involvement
- Loser, why bother, apathetic attitude
- There are only thirteen clubs other than band, football, etc.
- Low attendance at school
- Substance abuse substitutes for school involvement
- Wrong measures of success used

Solutions

- Build community support, sell the community.
- Analyze the master schedule–does it support participation in multiple activities?
- Investigate the impact of local requirements.
- Build tutorials and opportunities for participation into the school day.
- Look at other schools for best practices.
- Make students aware of the benefits of participating in activities.
- Close the campus.
- Change the policy to support desired outcomes, i.e., under current policy, a student is better off absent than tardy.

While action planning is not normally viewed as an orientation activity, it has been included here under orientation because in an open organization, changing the behaviors of current job holders is critical to restructuring the school district. By giving all school personnel up-front participation in the action planning, commitment to the plans is much more likely. Below are some participant reactions to the day's activities:

- I felt like we were a group that had one thing in mind–how to improve Pampa High School. It was like coaches planning for a major game. People from different areas of education were putting their heads together to accomplish one goal: a better education for our young people.
- I feel good that everyone now has a better understanding of the problems that everyone else is facing. I am disappointed that we did not have enough time to develop a complete written plan before we left.

- Many problems can be solved in this school district if we continue to have meetings with a similar format.
- I feel very positive and hopeful for the future. I just hope our work isn't put in a drawer and forgotten.
- The retreat was open, frank, and honest. I felt most of the people were willing to discuss the issues honestly. There were some whom I felt were still intimidated and did not express their true feelings.
- I feel very positive about the day's activities. The camaraderie and the group's desire to bring about change is exciting.

Maintenance

Six Steps to Succeed with Action Plans

While the workshop above created an excellent start for action planning, maintenance activities were necessary in order to foster the momentum. Consequently, the following information was circulated shortly after the workshop. "Establishing a process to achieve our strategic objectives is critical to the overall success of our strategic plan. Our four objectives are aggressive, but they can be achieved:

- "By 1990 to improve the self-esteem of all students by an average of 10 percent
- "To graduate all entering high school freshmen in increasing increments of 80 percent by 1992, 90 percent by 1996, and 100 percent by the year 2000
- "To have at least five National Merit Semi-Finalists or Finalists in each Senior Class by 1993
- "Beginning in 1995, to involve 95 percent of the Pampa High School graduates in post-secondary education or gainful employment

"They can be achieved because of the value that we place on succeeding with every child, on the skills we have for facilitating the success of our teachers, and because of the attention we give to following a useful system for developing effective plans:

1. Determine the Outcome

- Clarify, review, and edit the action plans. The plans developed in the workshop need to be carefully reviewed for their content – do they consist of enough action steps to clearly describe what is to be accomplished?

- Set the outcomes. What is the specific outcome of the action plan? Outcomes indicate what is to be desired. Specifically, what will have been accomplished – what will be different? – when the action plan is completed?
- Determine when and how outcomes will be measured. This involves setting specific standards against which actual progress will be measured. The standards indicate what will be measured and when it will be measured. They are to be written, specific, realistic, and measurable. Sources of information are to be identified.

2. Schedule the Action Plans

- Break the action step down into a series of events or mileposts.
- Place a time estimate on the activity required to move from one event to the next.
- Determine which action steps and/or events must be done in sequence and which ones can be parallel with or independent of one another.
- Determine the sequence of events that comprises the longest length of time. This is the critical path that must be followed.

3. Provide for Adequate Control and Accountability

- Decide what kind of decisions are needed, when they are needed, and where in the organization they should be made.
- Determine who will review actions taken, to ensure that they are of appropriate quality.
- Clarify who will see that the action steps/events are actually accomplished.

4. Define Resources Needed to Support the Action Plans

- Calculate what resources are needed in terms of numbers of people, estimated hours, training, materials, equipment, etc.

- Consider who will do what for how long and with what resources.

5. Review the Plan's Action Steps and Resource Commitments

- How does the plan relate to other events and activities? Will modifications be needed?
- Will follow-up planning be required?
- Are there some other operational areas that need to be changed as a result of this plan? If so, when?

6. Commit to the Plan

- Provide the daily leadership which models belief in the importance of the plan.
- Keep the plan in the forefront.
- Celebrate success along the way!"

Many planning models stop at this point. However, attempting to restructure an open system such as a school district requires attention to additional factors. Consequently, the following checkpoints were covered in a workshop for the leadership team, which consisted of teachers, administrators, and counselors:

Testing the Soundness of Planning

(1) Check for consistency with the principles of participatory management.
(2) Check for consistency with the following strategic parameters:
   - "We will never allow failure to be final for any student."
   - "We will always base major program changes on current, accurate, and sufficient data to justify the changes."
(3) Employ the rules for planning:
   - Grocery Store Rule—Is the sequence of activities logical?
   - Efficiency Rule—Are any efforts redundant? Are similar efforts grouped together?
   - Is Anyone Home Rule—Is the planning sensitive to the availability of key equipment, facilities, and personnel?
   - Decision-Making Rule—Does it meet key event deadlines (the end of one plan may be the beginning of another)? Does it recognize the impact of one decision on another (until A is finished, the next step, B, is unclear)?

(4) Consider politically sensitive matters.
- Have we "conditioned the turf"?
- Are the planning efforts sensitive to the reasons for opposition to change, to the need for further discussion and training, to giving staff the opportunity to participate?
- Are we a "shared responsibility team"(see Chapter 3)?
- Are the right groups of teachers, staff, and community citizens involved at the right stages of planning and implementation?

It should be remembered that although the above may sound like a centralized planning model, it was designed to aid planning at the individual building level. The above planning process and test were used in a workshop format in which the participants, using the problems/opportunities surfaced in an earlier workshop, fashioned a responsive plan. The plan was developed in the morning session, critiqued during lunch, and revised during the afternoon session. Here are a few evaluations of the workshop:

- I think we were "set up to fail" (in the A.M. session), but we did learn a great deal through the process.
- Having to do the campus plan twice was a good learning experience.
- Frustrated totally in the morning. Afternoon made sense. The total day involved a great deal of learning about the process and how to!
- The tasks done today in planning would be impossible by myself. Team is essential.
- Confusing morning, but greater understanding after 2nd time around.
- I learned the importance of complete planning. Delegating will be more necessary next year.
- This is difficult—very tiring. It would have been helpful if someone had gone through the plan to describe it more fully. This would have eliminated some frustrations.

Management of Information

In an open system, information must be managed both externally and internally. This might seem like a contradiction since the open system is by definition subject to both external and internal influences. However, the very fact that the system is open argues for a systematic process of managing information, recognizing that other information will also filter into the organization. With reference to the management of professional information, Pampa was able to give one teacher one period of released time to review articles and reports of research for distribution to faculty, administrators, counselors, and parents. As a reference point, she used the four objectives of the Pampa district, but generally the articles she chose were designed to advance teacher discussion in the total instructional process that was being developed in the district. At times these became the focus for further discussion and follow-up on local campuses, but this varied by campus. The main point was to keep current research and professional thinking in front of the decision makers—the teachers, parents, administrators, and counselors.

Another useful approach is to encourage principals as the instructional leaders to direct articles to specific teachers whom they either wish to influence or who they know are interested in the subject of the article. If this approach is followed, it is important that the principal pencil a note, underline the relevant parts of the article, and suggest a conference on the implications of the article for the teacher's situation. Further, the principal might wish to make a note on his calendar to inquire about the teacher's reaction to the article in a few days. Such a follow-up communicates to the teacher that the principal is genuinely interested.

Management of internal information is quite important, especially during a time of major change initiatives. Since the restructuring organization will be making a number of changes all at the same time, the chance for misunderstandings and/or inappropriate applications of a practice is substantial. Ideally, in an open organization the members would feel free to raise issues, request clarification, and so forth. However, during the time of transition from a bureaucratic organization to a restructured one, habits of compliance and conformity may prevail.

In Pampa, we found it necessary to formulate a District Communication Committee, composed of administrators, teachers, and counselors who met with the superintendent on a periodic basis. Many districts have what may appear to be similar committees—variously known as morale committees, communication committees, or rumor control committees. A key difference between those types of committees and what we fashioned in Pampa is that while the former are usually horizontal (e.g., composed only of one role group, usually teachers), the Pampa group was vertical.

A further difference is that while those groups usually only supply information to a specific question, in Pampa we attempted to take a developmental approach. By having all role groups in the district represented, we were able to more quickly get answers to questions as well as to make sure that all groups got similar answers to similar questions. Our developmental approach was illustrated in our efforts to use our answers to reinforce the principles of restructuring. Sample questions and answers appear below to illustrate the point.

Why is Baker school dismissing at 3:15 when the other schools are not?

This derived from the Baker School October self-esteem meeting and was voted on by the faculty. Several times the students were dismissed at 3:15. While we do want to encourage flexibility in individual campus decisions, the school day is so crowded that we need to be protective of student time in school. A student safety factor is also involved, as a student who gets hurt after being dismissed early could raise a liability issue. However, early dismissal of teachers after the school day is a decision of the campus principal and his local school committee. We have hard-working teachers throughout Pampa.

(NOTE—When campuses start to make individual decisions, it is inevitable that the variation in practices will be the subject of inquiry. Yet if campus decisions are to be encouraged, the early efforts must be supported.)

Why have the cafeteria menus gone to five sheets for one month?

Dr. Griffith explained that last year the menus had very small print, and the feedback from students was that they were difficult to read. The food service department was encouraged to make the menus more readable and more inviting to the students.

(NOTE—Significant here is that student feedback is attended to and acted upon.)

Can the appraisal pre-observation conferences be held at another time rather than 7:30 A.M.?

It should be an expectation that pre-observation conferences be scheduled during school hours. Dr. Griffith will visit with the appraisers and look into scheduling the conferences at appropriate times—especially for those with small children. There were 281 appraisals this year, and overall everything went very smoothly. There was more flexibility and understanding by the appraisers of what Pampa is trying to accomplish through training in learning styles, METS, and cooperative learning. Dr. Griffith explained that Pampa had for years only trained administrators, and now with METS training for teachers also they too know what is expected of the appraisal instrument.

(NOTE–Significant here is that the teachers have received the same training as the appraisers and that some decisions are still the call of the superintendent, e.g., the decision that conferences are to be held during school hours.)

Principles of Participative Management

The principles of participative management will ring strange in the ears of those still operating under a bureaucratic orientation. Yet they are absolutely essential if the district is to be restructured. They represent the core beliefs about organizational structure and the people in the organization that are requisite for successful restructuring. Below are the principles, with explanations.

Organizational Structure Varies

This will contradict much of the neatness of the bureaucratic organization in which uniformity is the typical pattern. However, the uniformity is required because of the concern for control. With the more flexible approach of participative management, the structure may be adapted to the needs and the interests and skills of the members of the organizational unit. The structure of the organizational unit serves the members of the unit and the clients, not the other way around.

The Person Doing the Job Is the Expert

Again, this principle is in direct opposition to the bureaucratic position that the experts devise the best way to do the job and tell others how to perform it. By contrast, the basis for this principle lies in the fact that the person closest to the job has the most data, and if he/she is informed of and committed to the goals of the organization and has the authority to make changes, this person will best know the modifications that need to be made.

Strategic Information Flows Downward; Operational Information Flows Upward

In part this is an extension of the above principle. In order for operational information to flow upward, there must be a belief that those closest to the job know best how to do it. If this were not the case, there would be no interest on the part of the subordinates in producing the information. Neither would the leaders have any interest in receiving it. However, in order for the most useful operational information to flow upward, the subordinates must know the overall direction of the organization, the strategic information.

Decisions Are Made at the Lowest Appropriate Level

This too is a logical result of the belief that the person closest to the job is the expert. From a bureaucratic framework, this principle makes no sense. Why have a hierarchy if those of high rank are not supposed to make all the decisions? Most of the members of the hierarchy reached their senior levels by doing well the jobs they held lower in the organization, so why shouldn't they tell their subordinates how to do these jobs in the best way? In fact, a leader may have gotten his/her position for any of a number of reasons other than expertise—political savvy, family or personal connections, luck, or people skills, for example. Or the leader may have expertise in one job, but not the many jobs found in the organization. Or the leader may have had skills in the job many years ago, but those skills may be quite dated now. At any rate, subordinate confidence, commitment, and entrepreneurship will never be fostered by top-down leadership. Further, as was pointed out above, the person closest to the job has the day-to-day experiences that are critical in making strategic adjustments in the performance of the job.

Participation Cannot Exceed Ability

While this might seem to be quite obvious, the implications for the restructuring organization are quite different than the implications for the bureaucratic organization. In the bureaucratic organization, this is the argument for top-down leadership. In the restructuring organization, the implication is that much time, effort, and energy must be expended on developmental activities for the subordinates. Not only is training and education provided in job-related areas, but they are also provided in more generic areas. For example, the more progressive companies are providing education in reading, writing, and math even though the specific job assignment of the person may not require further education in that area.

Accountability Is Commensurate with Authority

This may have a deceptively agreeable ring to the ear of the bureaucrat. It sounds like a bureaucratic principle. In many schools, however, teachers and others complain about accountability *without* authority. A good example is the required teaching behaviors that are specified in many states and on which teachers are evaluated. Teachers are expected to utilize these behaviors even if they feel they are more effective, given the subject and the students they have, using other behaviors. Yet the teachers are expected to produce learning gains implementing behaviors they think are inappropriate. This is accountability without authority. Many school districts will find a number of similar practices once they begin to apply this principle.

Implementing Participative Management

If participative management is to become more than a slogan, a definite structure must be developed in order to assure that it functions. A simplified typical organizational chart would usually take on the appearance shown in Figure 2. By contrast, in order to assist all personnel to understand the changes in Pampa, the organizational structure shown in Figure 3 was developed.

Several points of difference should be noted in the two figures. First, while the school board is shown at the top of Figure 2 and the teachers are at the bottom, in Figure 3 the local school leadership teams are at the top with the school board at the bottom. The leadership teams consist of the principal, teachers, and parents (students could also be included) at each building.

Another point is that Figure 3 shows a much flatter organization. That is, there are fewer levels of management in Figure 3 than in Figure 2. This permits a faster transmission of decisions and an easy inclusion of all who need to be involved in a particular decision. Further, it omits much of the bureaucracy found in taller organizations.

A third observation is that the superintendent does not make instruction/curriculum decisions in the absence of consultation with the instructional leadership council. Since all decisions in the district are made with respect to the four district goals, which are instructional in nature, few decisions are made by the superintendent alone. The instructional leadership council consists of the superintendent, the assistant superintendents, and principal and teacher representatives. This team considers matters of concern to the whole district that may come from individual schools or from the central office. All decisions are made through consensus. A typical agenda is shown in Table 10.

Several items distinguish this agenda from a typical meeting agenda. First, the Welcome is unusual. Normally, a meeting just starts; there is a presumption that all the participants are obligated to be there. Second is the Team Effectiveness Critique, a process

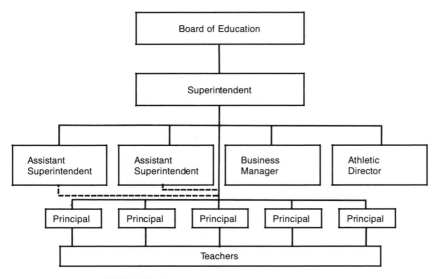

FIGURE 2. Traditional organizational chart.

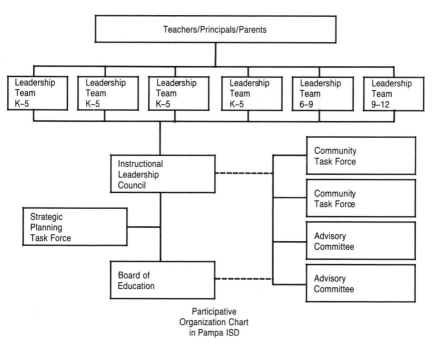

Participative
Organization Chart
in Pampa ISD

FIGURE 3. Participative organizational chart in Pampa ISD.

TABLE 10

12:30	Welcome
12:35	Team Effectiveness Critique
12:45	Review minutes from previous meeting
1:00	Pampa District Beliefs — "We hold these truths to be self-evident"
1:15	Technology Overview — "Where are we?"
2:00	Staff Development — Action Plan #3
	• Review plans • Small group discussion
	• Current status • Report back to large group
4:30	Adjourn

evaluation of the effectiveness of the previous meeting. This will be discussed further in the section below on Accountability. It is highly unusual for a group to reflect on the process of its deliberations.

A third unusual feature is the consideration of the beliefs of the district. This is critical because the beliefs of the district form the basis on which decisions are made for the district. Further, all of the issues before the group are instructional in nature, not management or administrative concerns. Finally, even though this was not solely a meeting on staff development, staff development considerations take a majority of the time of the meeting, reflecting the commitment of the district to developmental rather than judgemental approaches to the professional staff. It is also worth noting that this is the third try at devising an action plan; the district members have not been content just to adopt a standard one-day workshop approach. As in most of the meetings in Pampa, the meeting is structured so that small groups work and then report back to the whole group. This approach allows for maximum participation by all of the members of the group.

The local building leadership teams consist of the principal, and teacher and parent representatives. To get these started, Pampa adopted several non-negotiable requirements—they have to meet weekly; they have to construct the agenda at the meeting (rather than permitting the principal to construct it alone, a controlling signal); and the minutes must be posted for the entire faculty to read. Beyond this, the teams make recommendations to the instructional leadership council, consider proposals made by the council, and fashion local responses to opportunities in their own building.

Accountability

As treated in restructuring, accountability is critical for the organization, for it is through accountability that the organization becomes a *learning* organization. Sutherland [1] has described open-loop and closed-loop systems. Open-loop systems do not learn from previous experience. Thus, for the open-loop organization, each action starts from a blank tablet position. A good example is the organization that continues to have nonproductive meetings year after year.

Closed-loop organizations by contrast actively seek data from past events to guide them in present behavior. Closed-loop organizations are learning organizations since they are constantly seeking to improve their methods of operation. Since restructuring is essentially a self-taught process, it is critical that the organization be a closed-loop organization. While many organizations may utilize the outcomes of their decisions in order to make better decisions ("We lost that last attempt to fire a teacher. Next time we will have much improved documentation"), it is the rare organization that generates data about its *process* of operation. Yet, in an organization that is restructuring, such data are critical since the organizational members are attempting to learn new decision-making behaviors.

In Pampa, we utilized several approaches to generate data. For example, all workshops were evaluated, but not with the typical evaluation approach that lets participants merely put a check in a blank ("This workshop was Excellent, Good, Fair, Poor" or "The presenter was Very Knowledgeable, Somewhat Knowledgeable, Not at All Knowledgeable"). By contrast, in Pampa, we requested responses on the part of the participants. Below are sample questions that might appear on such a response form:

- Write a statement that describes your feelings regarding the day's activities.
- Describe any insights, skills, or information that increased in meaning for you today.
- Reflecting on the day, what activity was most useful to you? Why?
- Reflecting on the day, what activity was least useful to you? Why?
- Do you have any other comment, reaction, or suggestion?

A response form such as this generates a rich body of data that can assist the planner in knowing what was learned, what has been confused, and what was totally missed. The planner can then know the content and the preferred format for the next meeting. Another form that was used at all instructional leadership council meetings is the team effectiveness critique, shown in Appendix L.

The value of this form is that it permits the group to track the effectiveness of its processes. At each meeting the results of the previous meeting were reported and reflected upon, especially if the results were sharply out of line with previous results or if improvement was indicated. Since the group was learning to make decisions by consensus, feedback on performance was critical to developing a more effective group.

A third type of accountability was the end-of-year assessment. All units of Pampa completed a reflective document similar to the one in Appendix M, which was completed by members of the instructional leadership council (sample responses are also included).

Troubleshooting

It seemed to me that the main point of your section on building the flexible, responsible organization was writing a job description. Frankly, I didn't see much difference between the job description process you favored and the one that was taken from the consulting group.

There were several key differences. First, the individual himself was writing his own job description; it was not drafted by experts. A second difference is that it was to be written with reference to the mission of the organization, which had been fashioned with much participation by all parties, including the board and the community. A third difference is the emphasis on results. Of the six parts of the job description process, five focus on results. This is entirely in line with the restructuring emphasis on accountability with authority.

The planning model you described in your section under "Maintenance" sounded very similar to the one we use in my district. I'm assuming there is a difference, but if there is, it escaped me.

While I am not familiar with your particular planning model, I can guess that it is a very linear bureaucratic model. There are several differences between the model we have followed and the typical linear model. First, keep in mind that the planning process was to facilitate planning at the building level; it was not a master plan for the entire district. Second, there was to be wide-ranging participation in the shaping of the plan. Third, recall that there was a process for testing the soundness of the planning that acknowledged the fact that the organization is an open organization subject to many external, as well as internal, influences. Fourth, keep in mind that the planning process begins only after a mission has been committed to, team-building and consensus decision making have been well-established, and all parties understand that the planning process will result in definite action. It is not too much to say that the success of the planning process is directly related to the thoroughness of the activities prior to the initiation of that process.

With all due respect, some of the evaluations you reported were not all that complimentary. What makes you so sure your planning was a success?

As was discussed in Chapter 3, conflict is to be expected in a healthy organization. While the positive evaluations far outnumbered the negative, we wanted to be fair and report there were negative reactions. We were pleased with how many of the participants reported about the openness and honesty in the group.

I took exception to the organizational chart you used showing the school board at the bottom of the process. Point of fact, as I am sure you know, the board is the legal authority for the district. No matter how you draw that chart, they are the final decision makers. And in your own discussion of participative management, you said that strategic information flows down the organization.

The last comment in your question makes the point we wish to underline. Yes, policy *may* originate from the board. On the other hand, in the restructured organization, many suggestions for policy may begin with a teacher noting a need for change. But even if all policy were to originate with the board, that would represent a small portion of the business of the district. To place the board at the top sends the wrong message to the rest of the members of the educational enterprise (administrators, teachers, parents, students, the community at large) about their worth and value.

Reference

1. Sutherland, J. 1975. *Systems Analysis, Administration and Architecture*. New York: Van Nostrand.

⑧ Considerations in Restructuring

Several key issues continue to surface in restructuring. Not only must the leader have information about these matters, but he must see how these issues are related to the total organizational structure he is building. In some circles, choice is synonymous with restructuring. Former Secretary of Education Cavazos, for example, has frequently used the terms interchangeably. Another issue sure to come up is the issue of budget – how much control should the campus have, and what percent should be exclusively determined by the individual campus? Staff development is a third area that is frequently mentioned in conjunction with restructuring. What is the best way to foster staff development at the campus level? Personnel is yet another area of interest in restructuring, and a final area is accountability. How can the individual campus be held accountable without imposing a straightjacket on planning at the campus level?

Choice

While choice is not necessarily linked to restructuring, this connection has increasingly been made by politicians and businessmen. The reasons for this appear to be their desire to bring market forces to bear in education. Choice, they argue, would force schools to improve or go out of business. There would be rewards for the successful and therefore more incentive for other schools to adopt the successful practices or experiment to create more successful practices of their own. Logically as well, it is argued, choice would be linked with restructuring, for with increased autonomy in decision making would come increased diversity in schools. Parents would likely expect to exercise choice with respect to that diversity.

Those who would argue against choice fear that the choice would be exercised largely by middle-class parents while the poor and those traditionally not well-served by schools would get what was left. They

161

argue that all schools should be improved, thus rendering choice unnecessary. A panel for the Association for Supervision and Curriculum Development, for example [1] has questioned whether education is a public or private good. If public, then logically choice should not be permitted. If private, then choice would be quite defensible. Related issues they cite are whether good students should be permitted to gravitate to certain schools, leaving other students to languish with no peer models, and whether some schools should be permitted to receive private funds over and above the publicly allocated funds.

It seems that offering choice would create competition between schools and that this competition could be quite helpful in bringing improved services to students. At the same time, choice could create a bureaucratic nightmare as complicated controls and safeguards are developed to ensure equity and fairness. Bureaucracy is the very organizational design that restructuring is intended to diminish, not increase. The two options that have emerged to introduce market forces to education are either choice (favored by the Bush administration and businessmen) or broad community participation in setting the goals for schools and developing the plans for implementation (as in Pampa, for example). Perhaps the best one can do at this time is to be well-informed on the issues and be guided by dedication to providing the best educational opportunities for all students.

Scholarly Responses to Issues in Choice

Bastian [2] provides a definition of choice, as "a system of unzoned, competitive enrollments in place of neighborhood schools." She goes on to state that schools would compete with one another to attract students. Clinchy [3] enlarges the Bastian definition by noting that choice would apply not only to parents, but also to teachers and principals. That is to say, teachers and principals could move to schools that would design programs in line with their philosophies of education. As Clinchy notes, "If schools are to be given autonomy, we are all going to have to abandon our notion that there is one best way to educate young people. Rather, there are many avenues to education that will develop over a period of years." Indeed, in describing a parent choice plan that has been in place for seventeen years, Lambert and Lambert [4] chronicle the addition and deletion of several distinctive schools from which parents could choose.

The issue of the source of choices has received attention. Some [5,6] suggest that educators in autonomous buildings should create distinctive programs from which parents would select. Others [7,8] hold that parents should be a part of the decision-making process in creating the options from which choices will be made available. In discussing how vanguard companies respond to customer needs, O'Toole [9] describes these companies as listening with a third ear. He notes that customers never requested DuPont to invent nylon; however, they were quite vocal about the problems posed by silk. It was then up to the scientists and engineers to develop the product that would meet consumer requirements. Turning to education, parents might very well state their concerns with current education offerings; it would be up to professional educators to create responses to parent concerns. For some, however, such a scenario creates the image of schools as loose cannons, each going its own way with little quality control. As Glenn [10] says, "Parents should be assured there are no poor choices." To assure this, there must be a statement of broad goals that all schools will be expected to pursue [11,12].

A number of the benefits of choice have been cited. Clinchy [13] has suggested that choice is the best hope of changing the way schools are run—from bureaucratic organizations to responsive, client-oriented ones. Lambert and Lambert [14] have noted that voters in a choice district approved a tax increase by a 72 percent margin, at a time when most districts in California were turning tax increases down. Nathan [15] reports that choice has produced dramatic benefits in student achievement, parent satisfaction, and feelings of professional fulfillment by teachers and administrators.

Others have expressed alarm at the problems posed by choice. Bastian [16] expresses concern about matters such as equity; the many real problems of schools that choice will not address such as funding, poor facilities, and equipment; the need for teacher upgrading; the lack of parent involvement if the chosen school is distant from the neighborhood; the possibility of shifts in student enrollment requiring (unwilling) teacher transfers; the possibility that schools will attempt to maintain enrollments through marketing ploys rather than genuine improvements in education; and the draining of funding from other programs to permit funding of the increased expenses necessitated by choice programs. Lambert and Lambert [17] note that choice programs increase administrative problems, make district-wide coordination and articulation more difficult, and escalate costs. A report by the Council of Chief State School Officers on magnet schools provides disturbing information about equity and costs [18]. They report that magnet schools are creating a two-tiered system of haves and have nots. Further they report that the magnet schools receive additional funding and staffing. Magnet schools would not work without the additional resources, they found. While school choice is not necessarily linked to magnet schools, the principle of choice has been tested in these schools and found wanting. This report verifies that the problems cited by other writers are real and points out that a sound plan must be in place in order for choice plans to be successful.

Guidelines that will aid the success of choice plans have been suggested by Bastian [19] who calls for intra-district choice, a districtwide school improvement effort, school collaboration rather than school competition, high equity standards, sufficient funding, and linkage of schools to parents and home communities. Clinchy [20] holds that to be successful, choice plans must incorporate the following: genuine diversity between schools, autonomy for individual schools, educational equity for all students but especially poor and minority students, and a shift in the role of central administration from directing to coordinating.

Nathan [21] has offered the following guidelines:

- Include a clear statement of the goals and objectives that all schools are expected to meet.
- Encourage many educators within a given geographical area to develop distinctive schools and assist them in doing so, rather than simply concentrating resources on a few schools (e.g., creating magnet schools).
- Provide information and counseling to help parents select among various programs.
- Avoid first come-first served admissions procedures.
- Make transportation within a reasonable area available for all students, with a priority given to those coming from low-income and non-English-speaking families.
- Do not allow admission to schools on the basis of past achievement or behavior.
- Develop and follow racial balance procedures that promote integration.
- Require that dollars follow students.
- Include provisions for detecting oversights and for making continuing modifications.

Uchitelle [22] offers the following suggestions: equitable access as long as racial balance can be maintained, complete transportation services, and one choice per child to prevent school hopping. Certainly there are many cautions to be observed in developing a choice plan.

Broad community participation both in setting the goals for education and developing plans for implementation may achieve the benefits of a market orientation without some of the problems posed by choice plans. It may also achieve the benefit supported by Glenn [23] of assuring parents that there are no bad choices. A detailed account of this approach was presented in Chapter 5. The benefits of a market orientation may well be worth the difficulties. After seventeen years of implementing a choice plan, Lambert and Lambert [24] conclude,

> We believe the criticisms and problem solving we experienced in Lagunitas are signs of a dynamic and democratic school community. Most important, the members of our community – students, parents, teachers, administrators, other staff members, school board members – all feel invested in our schools. Our success hinges on a sense of efficacy, self-direction, and a movement toward autonomy, growth, and informed choice. Many of us in the Lagunitas school community feel that is what schools in a democratic society are all about.

Budget

"The first thing we had to deal with was budget. At first we allowed part of the budget to be decided at the school level, but we didn't make any real progress until we put the whole budget at the school level" [25]. This comment by the superintendent of the Edmonton Public Schools highlights the potential significance of participation in budget matters. With the shift of budget would come a shift in power. David Kearns [26], CEO of the Xerox Corporation, for example, has proposed that the individual schools compare the costs of central office services to competing suppliers or other potential uses of that money. Currently, no district has taken such a radical approach to budget decentralization, but Kanter [27] reports that a number of corporations are following just such a policy. Units within a corporation decide how much accounting services they want, how much help from sales, and so forth. Further, they are free to put services out for bids, in competition with similar services available within the corporation. With no unit in a corporation assured of the business of the other units in the business, she reports a noticeable shift to serving the needs of the other units in the organization, rather than merely protecting turf. Returning to budgeting in the schools, some have suggested that central purchasing, payroll, and other similar services would be maintained at the central office to achieve economy of scale, with most other budget lines allocated to the schools to do with as they see fit. Much flexibility could emerge in such a system with great vitality for the educational program for children.

Staff Development

Staff development has been called the slum area in education. In spite of the fact that the one-day seminar has little effect on teaching practice, that continues to be the dominant pattern in staff development. Even well-intentioned efforts that tried to utilize information on effective staff development have enjoyed little success. Early research typically focused on in-service presenters, who had the most credibility with teachers, the most effective delivery systems, favored locations, and the most effective patterns. The outcomes of this research found that practicing teachers had by far the most credibility with other teachers, followed by change agents and experienced college professors. Preferred locations were in the building. Effective patterns tended to be those emphasizing self-instruction, those that placed the teacher in an active role, and those offering choice.

The outcome of staff development based on such research was summarized by Boschee and Hein [28]. They conducted an evaluation of a workshop immediately after it was completed, in which 97 percent of the teachers said they would recommend the workshop. Six months later the researchers conducted a follow-up evaluation, and not only found no change in the target teacher behaviors, but also found a shift in attitude so that only 40 percent of the teachers said they would recommend the workshop and further that 20 percent of the teachers said they would not recommend the workshop under any conditions. Teacher complaints that surfaced in the six months follow-up, considered in conjunction with the researcher observations, are instructive about the defects of even the best workshops such as this one. Some weaknesses noted were that it covered too much material; more relevant classroom examples were needed; it focused on the teaching of skills rather than a conceptual understanding; it used a one-shot approach; and it was totally structured so that participants could not modify techniques or goals.

Current Research Findings

Subsequent research has shifted attention to more productive lines of inquiry—adult learning preferences, models of effective change, and combinations of approaches. Adult learning preferences include the following:

- Adults reject prescriptions from others for their learning.
- Adult learning is highly ego-involved. They tend to resist any learning experiences that they believe constitute either

open or implied attacks on their personal or professional
competence.

- Adults need to see the results of their efforts and have
  frequent and accurate feedback about progress that is being
  made.
- Adults will learn when the goals and objectives of all
  learning activities are considered by the learner to be
  realistic, related, and important to a specific issue.
- Adult motivation comes from the learner and not from any
  external source. Adults want to be the origins of their own
  learning.
- Adults come to any learning experience with a wide range of
  previous experiences, knowledge, skills, and competencies.
  Development activities should aim to build on these [29].

Several models for effective change have been validated in research. Joyce and Showers, for example, proposed the following:

- presentation of theory or description of a skill or strategy
- modeling or demonstration of the skill or strategy
- practice in simulated and classroom settings
- structured and open-ended feedback (e.g., provision of
  information about performance)
- coaching for application (e.g., hands-on, in-class assistance
  with the transfer of skills and strategies to the classroom)
  [30]

Glickman presented a summary of major findings:

- Participants should be involved in the planning.
- Planning should be for the long term.
- Released time should be provided for participants.
- Training should be concrete and specific.
- The training should be provided in small group workshops.
- Peer observations and feedback should be provided.
- Demonstration, trial, and feedback in workshops should be
  provided.
- Regular participant meetings should be planned for after
  the initial training and practice for problem solving,
  experimentation, and alterations should be arranged.
- Instructional and school leaders should participate in the
  activities [31].

Bernice McCarthy has formulated a staff development system
based on learning style research, brain dominance research, and the

research of the stages of concern that individuals move through as they are involved in an innovation. Her idea is that staff development should be compatible with these three aspects of a teacher's cognitive framework if it is to make sense to them and have a chance of making an impact.

Combining these three research thrusts, she has developed a sequence that all staff development should follow. First should come an awareness of and information about the innovation, followed by the teachers developing their own personal meanings. Once this is done, they should move to issues of management, first using a cookbook approach and then gradually proceeding to making a unique adaptation of the innovation. When the adaptation has been in place for sufficient time they should reflect on the outcomes of the adaptation, and finally they should become consultants to other teachers about the innovation [32].

Showers, Joyce, and Bennett present a meta-analysis of over 200 research studies on staff development, with the following points highlighted:

- What the teacher thinks about teaching determines what the teacher does when teaching; therefore, we must do more than go through the motions of teaching.
- The Joyce-Showers training model provides a useful basis for designing staff development.
- Teachers with high self-esteem usually benefit more from training. Coaching helps teachers utilize the new practice.
- Teachers who are flexible in their thinking are quicker to use new skills.
- Teaching styles and value orientations do not influence their ability to utilize training.
- Initial enthusiasm in training does not indicate later level of usage.
- Teacher participation in the organization of the training does not influence the effectiveness of the staff development activity [33].

Much of the research above, however, is tied to the bureaucratic model, tacitly making several assumptions about staff development. For example, these authors assume that staff development will be districtwide because the necessary planning would be cost-prohibitive otherwise and that it will be planned from the top and presented by someone alien to the school building since most teachers would lack the sophistication required by many of these systems. Even in those instances in which choice is endorsed, the menu of choice is typically seen to come from the top. Some common presumptions regarding staff development are that teachers are deficient and need a skill in which they can be trained, that research has discovered that skill, and that this training will provide that skill. Others seem to feel that teacher commitment is not necessary or that it can be whipped up by a skillful trainer, that there is no necessary connection between staff development and the school vision and mission that the teachers have exercised a major role in developing, and that there is no moral dimension in teaching.

Among the more condescending assumptions are that teacher judgement is not a major factor in teaching and that there is no cognitive aspect to staff development and teaching—just put together a training package based on research-validated principles and plug the teachers in (and oh, yes, make some allowance for adult learning preferences, learning styles, and stage of concern). These assumptions must be put to rest quickly if progress is to be made in effective staff development in restructured schools.

Problems with the staff development assumptions are obvious, and solutions can be found. Rather than having staff development on a district level, it must occur and be planned at the building level. This follows because the building has developed its concerns and has made a commitment to attack those concerns. Teachers will be very active in planning the staff development needs because these needs will naturally grow out of the ongoing review of what the teachers are trying to accomplish and where they presently are in that process. Teachers should not be viewed as deficient; rather, the attitude should be that they are constantly improving as their view of their purpose and their positions in relation to that purpose become increasingly clear. This reflects the conviction of those engaged in restructuring that those closest to the job know best how to do that job and what they need to do it better.

Teacher commitment is absolutely essential if improvement is to occur. However, the artificial commitment observed at the close of some staff development sessions is not what is sought but, rather, the commitment that grows out of deeply held beliefs about the mission of the school, and the moral imperative of teaching. Many trainers will acknowledge that teacher judgement is a factor in teaching. On the other hand, few trainers are prepared to accept a teacher judgement that their particular training package is not appropriate for the teacher's situation. Further, few staff developers would be able to acknowledge that the high-priced trainer they brought in did not present material relevant to the needs of the teachers!

Many training sessions will provide at least some nominal amount of time for teachers to reflect on the content of the training session. However, the reflection tends to be superficial in the absence of any shared vision, a moral view of teaching, and a commitment to achieving the mission of the school.

Staff Development in Restructured Schools

From the assumptions of current staff development programs and the responses to those assumptions above, the essentials of a staff development program can be derived. First, don't abandon everything that has preceded the staff development sessions. This one dictum requires that it grow from the efforts to improve programs at the building level, that it relate directly to the vision and mission of the school, that it build on the commitment of the teachers already in place, and that it be very respectful of the talent and skill of the teachers. Second, understand that much of the "staff development" will not look like staff development. That is to say, it may take the form of a teachers' meeting to discuss problems and possible responses to those problems, hammering out organizational changes that will help further the educational goals of the school, developing a parent assistance program, sharing articles or concepts from a professional meeting, reassessing the vision or mission of the school, reflecting on research on human cognition or curriculum/instruction, etc.

On occasion, an outside expert may be brought in, but the emphasis will be on the expert's being responsive to the needs of the teachers, not on his presenting a canned training program. Teachers may visit other districts—not to bring back that program but to check the fit between that program and their own vision/mission. Structured opportunities for communication such as peer coaching, fireside chats, and mentoring will provide the stimulus for reflection and change. Teachers themselves will share successes they have had or that they have observed during a peer coaching session. In-house activities can fall flat on their face. They can be poorly planned, ineptly carried out, shallow in their conceptualization, lacking in follow-through, implemented just to meet a requirement or mandate, spiritless, and so forth. What can one do to prevent these very real possibilities?

Staff development can be inspiring and renewing. It can lead to recommitment and a renewed effort to find things that work. To reach these heights, staff development in restructured schools will grow from real needs that relate directly to the vision and mission of the school (a vision and mission shared by parents and students, as well as teachers and administrators), will be hammered out in the context of daily practice with feedback from peers, and will stay focused on improvement because of the moral basis of teaching. It will directly connect with the experiences of the teacher and will shape the instruction that pupils receive. To achieve these ends, a well-defined structure will be necessary.

A Structure for Staff Development

A structure that will provide the basis for meaningful staff development will start by keeping the vision and mission of the school at the center of the process. Needs with respect to these can be surfaced by a discrepancy analysis and action plan that focuses on "where we are and where we need to (would like to) be" (see Appendix N). Organizational structures as well as curricular, instructional, and discipline practices can come under scrutiny as alignment is sought between the vision/mission and practices. Key here is that there will be no sacred cows—anything can be subject to scrutiny. At this point one may wonder what is to keep the teachers from taking some safe (and easy) route by discovering a "need" for which there is a video available from the central office, scheduling the video, and calling the required staff development a done deal. This is unlikely to occur because of their commitment to the vision/mission of the school and their elevated view of teaching as a profession.

Personnel

In the restructured school, teachers will exercise their judgement regarding a number of issues that have traditionally been the concern of the personnel department. Areas such as staff development—which was discussed above—will become the concern of the local building. Other areas include recruitment, selection, and induction. In the future, appraisal and compensation could also become building-level responsibilities, but at present these two appear more distant. As schools become more accountable for achieving their outcomes, they will increasingly become more active in recruitment in order to attain the personnel most likely to help them achieve their mission. As in so many instances in restructuring, recruitment should be continuous and should start at the campus level.

For example, the substitute might be persuaded to get an emergency certificate and work toward certification. The sons or daughters of faculty members might be encouraged to teach for a year or two. Professional conferences can be the occasion for telling about the unique focus of one's school to a prospective recruit. Student teachers are an obvious possibility, and parents who assist in the school might be a good bet. Previous graduates of the school could be tracked and urged to return to the home school, and teachers' friends, neighbors, and fellow church members are other possible candidates.

The point is that recruitment should not be left to someone else. Probably no one will be more concerned about the school meeting its mission than those most directly connected with the school. Once a large pool of candidates is developed, selection is the next task. If the school district already has an application blank, the school might consider developing a supplementary one that will supply information considered essential because of the mission of that school. A profile of the effective faculty member will have been prepared in advance, and screening on the basis of this profile can narrow the pool of candidates to a few. Teachers will need to be included at every stage of the process since they are selecting a colleague. Rather than having the teacher candidate face a group of teachers all at once, which might be intimidating, arrangements can be made for the candidate to meet with teachers individually. Reactions can be gathered from the teachers individually or as a group as they share perceptions.

Once the candidate has been selected, induction should begin. A letter from the teachers who will be working with the new teacher is a good idea. Information on the community, the school, and the district can be forwarded. Socials early in the year can help the candidate feel welcome. Teachers have told of having no introduction to the faculty at all except for the formal introduction at the beginning of the year. Since a restructured school is a school in which much group communication is fostered, induction activities that insure a warm welcome to the new teacher are well-advised.

The new teacher to the system will need a mentor teacher, which is not to be confused with the buddy teacher that is typically assigned. The buddy teacher usually helps the new teacher with his questions, shows him/her how to fill out forms, advises about due dates, and so forth concerning the mechanics of getting started. That is about the extent of the buddy teacher responsibilities. The mentor teacher, on the other hand, assists the teacher recruit in learning the norms of the school, the informal rules that define best practice; alerts him/her to taboos; helps with the early discipline questions; and generally functions as insurance that the teacher makes a good start. Mentors usually assume responsibility for the new teacher's success in fact if not as a requirement of the role.

Principals also have to attend to the care and feeding of the new teacher. Under current practice in many schools the principal may not even check with the new teacher unless there are signs of trouble. In restructured schools, by contrast, the principal may be in the new teacher's room every day for the first month. Professionals in restructured schools are not willing simply to shrug and assume that the first-year teacher is going to have a difficult time. When the whole school is accountable, one cannot write off even one teacher. Beyond the accountability issue, however, is the view of teaching as a moral act and the vision and mission of the school to which the teachers, parents, and students are deeply attached.

Appraisal and Compensation

Appraisal and compensation are probably going to be somewhat more distant responsibilities for the local school than those listed above; therefore, only a few observations will be offered. As the mission of the school becomes more clearly etched, inevitably, the school will need its own appraisal system. If schools are required to use a state-developed form, schools may wish, in addition, to develop one of their own that more nearly reflects the commitments of the staff, parents, and students of that school.

Guidelines that may influence the development of that system may be drawn from the critique of many state-mandated forms of teacher evaluation and a distinctly different view of teaching proposed by Shulman, who has developed standards for the National Board of Professional Teaching Standards [34]. In his critique, Shulman notes that most of the state-mandated evaluation forms are heavily oriented toward scientific management. These systems require that teaching be defined in terms of generic teaching behaviors and that they be phrased exclusively in terms of observable classroom behaviors. Shulman and his colleagues reason that this view of teaching is too simplistic. Rather, they hold that teaching varies with the subject, the purpose, the students, and the level. Further, they argue that teaching is an intellectual and imaginative process, not merely a behavioral one. They suggest that it is at least as important for teachers to be able to explain the reasons for their choices as it is to engage in appropriate teaching behavior.

Using these views as a guideline, appraisal in restructured schools might take the form of a meeting where the teacher discusses with a peer observation team the reasons for his/her teaching decisions, with respect to the mission/vision of the school. In addition, the teacher might submit a portfolio of teaching materials, submit a videotaped lesson with explanations for teaching decisions, and perhaps take a written test or submit a written statement regarding the implications of the school's mission/vision for his/her practice as a teacher.

At any rate, it appears clear that the scientific management driven appraisal systems that many states have adopted cannot assist teacher growth in the areas required for effectiveness in a restructured school. A system that fosters the development of a view of teaching more in line with that being recommended to the National Board of Professional Teaching Standards by Shulman will aid appraisal in the restructured school.

Differentiation in compensation for teachers is already a fact in any districts. If the personnel principle of giving the most children contact with the best teachers is to be followed, then it appears inevitable that some sort of differentiated staffing such as that supported by the Carnegie Foundation through the National Board of Professional Teaching Standards will be found in restructured schools. Writing on compensation plans developing in post-entrepreneurial corporations, Kanter [35] observes that they are adopting a multi-faceted approach reflecting the various emphases of the corporation. Thus they may have a small base pay, with opportunities for bonuses for individual productivity, company profitability, and contributions to the team.

Assuming that restructured schools would take on the compensation trends of corporations, it is not too much to imagine teachers receiving a base salary with some adjustments for variations in responsibility, with bonuses for gains by their students in defined areas (this issue will be discussed below under Accountability), for school gains in these same areas, and for their contributions to the team. If schools follow industry trends as described by Kanter, there is little doubt that there will be a shift from compensation strictly based on job title to compensation based on a mix of factors, including outcomes.

Accountability

The heart of the move toward restructuring is the belief that if a school is truly to be held accountable for outcomes, then it must have the flexibility to develop its own program. So long as schools must implement programs mandated by others, even if school personnel have deep philosophical differences with those programs, little commitment can develop. Further, holding one school accountable for another's notion of what works appears patently unfair. Thus it seems that restructuring and accountability are inexorably linked. In a related vein, some hold that if choice becomes the dominant feature in restructuring, then accountability will take care of itself. David Kearns, for example, of the Xerox Corporation has said that the poor-performing schools will improve or go out of business, just as happens in private industry. If this is to work, however, schools will still need to provide the hard data on which parental decisions will be made.

If accountability and choice are to work for the improvement of education, several factors must change. First, the individual school must, in response to a community-identified set of goals, clearly define what its objectives are and how it intends to meet those objectives. At that point the parents can decide whether they think the objectives stated will lead to the goals identified by the community and whether the processes devised will lead to attainment of those objectives. Next, the schools must identify the measures they will use to judge the degree to which they have met their objectives. Considering the public expectations at this time, the measures should be standardized.

At present, virtually the only measures offered to the public are short-answer achievement tests in the basic subject areas. Shortcomings of such tests have been detailed by other authors. Suffice it to say that for the most part standardized tests measure low-level achievement in an artificial setting, that they are accorded far more credibility by the general public than they are by the test makers themselves, and that the unfortunate result of such heavy emphasis on one index of school effectiveness is to skew all school efforts toward raising test scores, thus ignoring other valid objectives of public schools. Further, by giving practice tests, teaching test-taking skills, and using other such devices, it is possible to raise test scores without increasing learning. Rather than succumb to the current status quo, restructured schools must become proactive in the matter of accountability.

In order to become proactive, restructured schools must go one step further after identifying their objectives and developing a plan for attaining those objectives. Restructured schools must identify, secure, utilize, and publicize standardized test scores for all of their stated objectives. For example, suppose a school has identified creativity, cross-cultural understanding, self-esteem, and problem solving as critical objectives, in addition to academic achievement. By using a standard reference source on mental measurements tests [36], the school should identify standardized measures, administer these, and publicize the scores.

This would have several salutary effects. First, it would assure parents that the school was quite serious about pursuing all of its stated objectives. Second, it would provide a standardized measure of the progress the students in the school were making toward attainment of the objectives. Third, it would provide a benchmark that would allow the parent to gauge the progress of his child with respect to the stated objectives. Fourth, it would help the school to identify areas in which extra energy or perhaps program revision or renewal were needed. In order to conserve academic learning time, the tests could be administered only to a sample of the students or to only a few grade levels on a staggered basis or they could be administered outside the regular school day.

Troubleshooting

I see two main problems in trying to implement a choice program— one internal and one external. The internal problem is, how do we prevent ambitious coaches from recruiting top athletes to their programs, circumventing the process by which parents and students would choose on the basis of academics? The other is, how do we get choice information to the parents of students who are traditionally poorly served by schools, so that they can make a good choice?

Both of these pose potential problems to the whole concept of choice, and policies need to be in place to ensure that choices are made for the right reasons. Turning to the internal problem first, some schools have provided for severe penalties, including firing the coach, in the case of coaches recruiting players. This may deter the coaches from recruiting but would not stop parents and students from selecting a school because of the reputation of a coach. This can be handled by requiring a player to sit out a season if he transfers from an unsuccessful program to one that has a better record.

With respect to the problem of getting information out to parents of poor and minority students, few answers are available. Contact with organized minority groups, churches, and social agencies that provide services the poor and minorities will make an effort to obtain, utilizing technology such as a recorded telephone message or a local television channel, and convincing local employers to allow their employees a day off, such as they allow for jury duty, are some ideas that have been tried in various communities. Keep in mind that choice will have been preceded by a community-wide discussion of school goals and will have attained broad-based support. Many civic groups may be interested in helping get the information out to parents who might not otherwise get enough information to make an informed choice.

I have real concerns about giving so much budgetary power to the individual schools. We have some pretty weak principals, and the union is pretty powerful. What is to prevent the principals and teachers from making decisions that are not in the best interests of the children?

Nothing, I suppose. On the other hand, the schools will be required to adopt explicit accountability measures and will be expected to show progress on those. Further, just suppose the teachers vote to give themselves a hefty raise and cut money for supplies. Who is to say that might not increase student achievement on the various accountability measures? A further check is that parents could be placed on the school governing council in addition to teachers and the principal. Ultimately, the schools must produce or lose students. Also, recall that the school will have adopted a mission and objectives to which they are deeply committed. Finally, recall that the superintendent of the Edmonton, Canada, schools has given full budget authority and says that was the beginning of true restructuring for them.

For a long time I have been stumped by our staff development program. We have tried a number of things and my impression is that little is different in the classroom because of them. Still, I am reluctant to turn everything over to the building. Somehow this seems like a cop out. Is there some way I can be sure that good staff development is taking place?

Yes. If activities are taking place that grow directly out of identified needs or problems in that school, then you can be sure that they are on the right track. There should be some process, formal or informal, that continually operates to assess teacher, curricular, instructional, or student needs. Further, there should be a group that has the responsibility for developing responses to those needs. This group should have minutes or other records of their deliberations and recommendations. Keep in mind that staff development in the restructured school may not always look like staff development. This same group should have a process of gathering data on the effectiveness of the staff development initiative, perhaps through peer observation, informal group meetings with teachers and students, or other methods. This information should be available to the superintendent. I must also observe, however, that your question betrays a hint of distrust in the local school to make professional decisions. If the proper groundwork has been laid, most schools will act in the best interests of the children.

Implementation Checklist

_____ 1. A clear policy exists on the matter of choice that addresses the issues raised in this chapter.

_____ 2. A clear process exists for gaining the involvement of minority and poor parents so they can make an informed choice for their children.

_____ 3. Safeguards have been built into the system to insure that equity is observed in assigning students. Particular care has been exercised in the matters of athletes and high-achieving students to insure they do not create pockets of privilege with children of poor and minorities getting what is left.

____ 4. Provisions for transportation have been made for those students who qualify on some objective basis (such as those on free or reduced lunch, for example).

____ 5. All possible budgetary decisions have been delegated to the individual schools, with the schools in turn purchasing any centralized services they choose.

____ 6. Training has been provided for the principal, teachers, and parents on the legal requirements regarding budget matters.

____ 7. An orderly process for making budgets at all campuses has been devised to assist in setting the tax rate, etc.

____ 8. All staff development is now delegated to the individual campus.

____ 9. Staff development is based on needs identified in a particular school.

____ 10. An orderly process exists for identifying staff development needs and planning responses.

____ 11. It is widely understood and expected that a large number of activities and experiences may serve as staff development vehicles.

____ 12. An orderly process exists for assessing the effectiveness of staff development activities with respect to their impact on classroom instruction.

____ 13. The community has been deeply involved in setting the goals of the district schools.

____ 14. Each school has prepared a set of objectives to meet those goals.

____ 15. Each school has developed a program that will lead to the attainment of those objectives.

____ 16. School patrons understand that the schools pursue a number of goals in a democratic society and expect the school to provide evidence, standardized evidence, that progress is being made on all of the goals.

____ 17. Schools use the outcomes of the assessments in #16 to review programs to increase effectiveness.

References

1. *Public Schools of Choice*. 1990. Alexandria, VA: Association for Supervision and Curriculum Development.

2. Bastian, A. 1989. "Response to Nathan: Choice Is a Doubled-edged Tool," *Educational Leadership*, 47:56.

3. Clinchy, E. 1989. "Public School Choice: Absolutely Necessary but Not Wholly Sufficient," *Educational Leadership*, 47:290.

4. Lambert, M. and L. Lambert. 1989. "Parent Choice Works for Us," *Educational Leadership*, 47:58-60.

5. Glen, C. 1989. "Putting School Choice in Place," *Educational Leadership*, 47:295-300.

6. Nathan, J. 1989. "More Public School Choice Can Mean More Learning," *Educational Leadership*, 47:51-55.

7. Clinchy, E. loc. cit.

8. Lambert, M. and L. Lambert. loc. cit.

9. O'Toole, J. 1985. *Vanguard Management*. Garden City, NJ: Doubleday and Co. Inc.

10. Glen, C. op. cit., p. 296.

11. Clinchy, E. loc. cit.

12. Glen, C. loc. cit.

13. Clinchy, E. loc. cit.

14. Lambert, M. and L. Lambert. loc. cit.

15. Nathan, J. loc. cit.

16. Bastian, A. loc. cit.

17. Lambert, M. and L. Lambert. loc. cit.

18. Council of Chief State School Officers. 1989. *Educational Effects of Magnet High Schools*. Washington, D.C.: The Council.

19. Bastian, A. loc. cit.

20. Clinchy, E. loc. cit.

21. Nathan, J. loc. cit.

22. Uchitelle, S. 1989. "What It Really Takes to Make School Choice Work," *Edcuational Leadership,* 47:301-303.

23. Glen, C. loc. cit.

24. Lambert, M. and L. Lambert. op. cit., p. 60.

25. Strembitsky, M. Presentation at *Association for Supervision and Curriculum Development 45th Annual Conference, San Antonio, TX, March 5, 1989.*

26. Kearns, D. 1988. "A Business Perspective on American Schooling," *Education Week* (April 20).

27. Kanter, R. 1989. *When Giants Learn to Dance*. New York: Simon and Schuster.

28. Boschee, F. and D. Hein. 1980. "How Effective Is Inservice Education?" *Phi Delta Kappan*, 61:427.

29. Wood, F. and S. Thompson. 1980. "Guidelines for Better Staff Development," *Educational Leadership*, 37:374-378.

30. Joyce, B. and B. Showers. 1980. "Improving Inservice Training: The Messages of Research," *Edcuational Leadership*, 37:379-385.

31. Glickman, C. 1990. *Supervision of Instruction: A Developmental Approach, 2nd edition*. Boston: Allyn and Bacon.

32. McCarthy, B. 1982. "Improving Staff Development through CBAM and 4MAT," *Educational Leadership*, 40:20-25.

33. Showers, B., B. Joyce, and B. Bennett. 1987. "Synthesis of Research on Staff Development: A Framework for Future Study and a State-of-the Art Analysis," *Educational Leadership*, 45:77-87.

34. Shulman, L. 1987. "Assessment for Teaching: An Initiative for the Profession," *Phi Delta Kappan*, 69:38-44.

35. Kanter, R. loc. cit.

36. Conoley, J. and J. Kramer, eds. 1989. *The Tenth Mental Measurements Yearbook*. Lincoln, NB: The University of Nebraska-Lincoln.

APPENDIX A

The Learning Climate Inventory

Directions: Circle a number or rate your school on a scale of 1 to 5, with a rating of 1 indicating that you strongly disagree that the statement is true of your school, and a rating of 5 indicating that you strongly agree that the statement is true of your school.

1. Collaborative Problem Solving and Decision Making

Effective schools have shared decision making and problem solving and a sense of collegiality among the staff.

1.1	1 2 3 4 5	Faculty or department meetings are often used for involving staff in solving problems.
1.2	1 2 3 4 5	The staff shares a sense of commitment and can describe school goals in specific, understandable terms.
1.3	1 2 3 4 5	The staff is involved in planning school improvement activities.
1.4	1 2 3 4 5	Staff members feel that they are an important part of the school and that what they do contributes to its effectiveness.
1.5	1 2 3 4 5	Staff members receive recognition for their accomplishments.
1.6	1 2 3 4 5	Staff members talk freely and openly with one another about school problems.
1.7	1 2 3 4 5	Few people ignore problems, refuse to do what needs to be done, or say, "It's not my job."

1.8	1 2 3 4 5	Teachers are encouraged to communicate concerns, questions, or constructive ideas to supervisors.
1.9	1 2 3 4 5	Students participate, where appropriate, in solving the problems of the school.
1.10	1 2 3 4 5	Staff members participate in decision making in the school.

2. Instructional Leadership

Effective principals identify staff strengths and potential, provide learning opportunities for the staff, and integrate instructional goals into as many activities as possible.

2.1	1 2 3 4 5	The principal[2] frequently observes classroom instruction—both informally and through scheduled observations of teacher performance.
2.2	1 2 3 4 5	The principal[2] regularly talks with teachers about instructional matters.
2.3	1 2 3 4 5	The principal communicates the belief that all students can learn.
2.4	1 2 3 4 5	Faculty of departmental meetings include discussions on how to improve instruction.
2.5	1 2 3 4 5	Time is provided regularly for teachers to share their successes, their materials, and the solutions they have found to classroom problems.
2.6	1 2 3 4 5	The principal[2] encourages teachers to be creative and to try new methods of instruction appropriate to the objectives being taught.
2.7	1 2 3 4 5	The principal[2] makes clear to the staff his or her expectations for meeting instructional goals.
2.8	1 2 3 4 5	The principal[2] provides feedback on staff performance.
2.9	1 2 3 4 5	The principal protects instructional time by controlling interruptions.

[2] Or an appropriate staff member who serves as instructional leader.

2.10   1 2 3 4 5   In-service experiences for staff are provided to meet identified needs.

3. High Expectations for Students

When the focus of the school is on student learning and student acceptance of responsibility, student achievement tends to increase while discipline problems tend to decrease.

3.1   1 2 3 4 5   Low-achieving students are given the opportunity to successfully answer questions in the classroom.

3.2   1 2 3 4 5   Student accomplishments are recognized and rewarded.

3.3   1 2 3 4 5   All students are expected to follow the same set of rules.

3.4   1 2 3 4 5   When making important decisions, the educational growth of students takes priority.

3.5   1 2 3 4 5   Students are held responsible for their actions.

3.6   1 2 3 4 5   Students' work is displayed prominently in classrooms, corridors, and cafeterias.

3.7   1 2 3 4 5   Students share the responsibility for keeping the school environment attractive.

3.8   1 2 3 4 5   Students are expected to master the basic skills at each grade level.

3.9   1 2 3 4 5   Teachers provide opportunities for all students to develop higher-order skills.

3.10   1 2 3 4 5   Students are encouraged to participate in classroom and school activities, regardless of sex, race, religion, socioeconomic status, or academic ability.

4. Developing a Safe and Orderly Environment

When roles and expectations are clearly understood, when classroom instruction is well organized, and when an attitude of respect for the individual is evident in the school, there is a healthy climate for learning.

4.1   1 2 3 4 5   Rules and expectations are clearly defined, stated, and communicated so that students, teachers, and parents know what is expected.

4.2   1 2 3 4 5   Where appropriate, students are involved in rule making.

4.3   1 2 3 4 5   Teachers spend time "teaching" rules and procedures to students.

4.4   1 2 3 4 5   A minimum number of good rules are made and enforced; unenforceable rules are eliminated.

4.5   1 2 3 4 5   Appropriate reinforcement is used to encourage the desired behavior.

4.6   1 2 3 4 5   Teachers make an effort to know and use the names of the students in their classrooms, as well as the names of others in the school.

4.7   1 2 3 4 5   Teachers show respect for students as individuals and for their cultural differences.

4.8   1 2 3 4 5   Rules apply to behavior that is directly related to the school or classroom, not to matters that are petty or personal.

4.9   1 2 3 4 5   Before the first day of school, teachers prepare plans for classroom management that include identifying expected behaviors and developing ways to teach rules and procedures.

4.10   1 2 3 4 5   Punishment is delivered in a way that indicates disapproval of inappropriate behavior without humiliating the student.

5. Curriculum and Instructional Practices

Well-planned curriculum and instructional practices that address different learning styles and develop both basic and higher-order skills are characteristics of effective schools.

5.1   1 2 3 4 5   Each teacher uses a variety of teaching strategies or models.

5.2   1 2 3 4 5   A student may be transferred from one teacher to another or from one program to another, depending upon the student's learning needs.

5.3   1 2 3 4 5   Teachers organize classroom instruction

		for the most effective use of time for learning.
5.4	1 2 3 4 5	Teaching methods and instructional materials build on what the student already knows.
5.5	1 2 3 4 5	Time is set aside for teachers to plan together and discuss instructional goals.
5.6	1 2 3 4 5	Teachers sequence learning activities so that students can experience success at each step.
5.7	1 2 3 4 5	Teachers include student use of higher-order skills in their lesson plans.
5.8	1 2 3 4 5	Teachers present, demonstrate, and/or explain new content and skills and check for student understanding.
5.9	1 2 3 4 5	Teachers assign independent practice activities such as seatwork and homework only after students have demonstrated understanding of a skill or concept.
5.10	1 2 3 4 5	Curriculum guides insure that teachers cover similar subject content at the same grade level.

6. Monitoring Student Performance

6.1	1 2 3 4 5	Appropriate interpretation of standardized test results are provided so that teachers can modify instruction to meet students' learning needs.
6.2	1 2 3 4 5	Teachers assign homework to reinforce learning.
6.3	1 2 3 4 5	Children with special problems are diagnosed, and help is provided in a manner that does not stigmatize them.
6.4	1 2 3 4 5	The testing program measures student acquisition of both basic and higher-order skills.
6.5	1 2 3 4 5	Teachers make sure students have mastered the prerequisites before moving on to teach new skills.
6.6	1 2 3 4 5	A variety of methods are used to assess student progress in basic skills—for ex-

ample, work samples, mastery checklists, teacher-made tests, and criterion-referenced tests.

6.7   1 2 3 4 5   Teachers tell students specifically what is correct or good about their work and specifically what is incorrect or needs improvement.

6.8   1 2 3 4 5   Teachers can state what their student learning objectives are for each lesson.

6.9   1 2 3 4 5   Teachers use appropriate evaluation methods to determine if the students have successfully met learning objectives.

6.10   1 2 3 4 5   Student assessment information is regularly used to give specific feedback to students and parents about student progress.

7. Involving Parents and the Community

Close home and community contacts enhance school problem solving. Parent involvement in student learning increases achievement.

7.1   1 2 3 4 5   Teachers and administrators are actively involved in groups and organizations within the community that can offer support to the school.

7.2   1 2 3 4 5   Community businesses are asked to be a part of the school—for example, by providing speakers, donating material and equipment, and serving on advisory committees.

7.3   1 2 3 4 5   Parents are treated courteously when they call or visit the school.

7.4   1 2 3 4 5   Parents are invited to visit classrooms to observe the instructional program.

7.5   1 2 3 4 5   A school newsletter or bulletin is sent regularly to parents to keep them informed about school activities, changes in rules or procedures, or on instructional matters.

7.6   1 2 3 4 5   Parents are informed at the beginning of the school year of school homework policies, and are asked to agree to supervise their children's homework.

7.7	1 2 3 4 5	Each teacher schedules at least one conference with the parents of each student in his/her class during the first half of the year.
7.8	1 2 3 4 5	Parents who work have the option of having parent-teacher conferences in the evening or by telephone.
7.9	1 2 3 4 5	Parents are included on school advisory committees.
7.10	1 2 3 4 5	Parent volunteers are used wherever possible—for example, as library aides, to help with instructional materials, or for hall or lunchroom duty, etc.—not just for fund-raising activities.

8. Physical Environment

Environments that are pleasant for adults and students to work in encourage learning.

8.1	1 2 3 4 5	Space is used efficiently for storing materials and equipment.
8.2	1 2 3 4 5	The school activities are arranged so that disturbing noises are kept to a minimum.
8.3	1 2 3 4 5	Classroom space is arranged so that students can work undisturbed.
8.4	1 2 3 4 5	The flow of traffic in the school is planned to allow easy movement within and between classrooms and large group areas.
8.5	1 2 3 4 5	There are quiet places where individuals may think, read, or work.
8.6	1 2 3 4 5	Classrooms and the library are arranged so that small groups can work together.
8.7	1 2 3 4 5	The walls of common areas and hallways are brightened by the use of student artwork.
8.8	1 2 3 4 5	Staff and students feel responsible for keeping the school environment attractive and clean.
8.9	1 2 3 4 5	Teachers have a comfortable, quiet area for planning.
8.10	1 2 3 4 5	The school grounds are kept free of litter.

This instrument was developed by Dr. Patricia C. Duttweiler (Southwest Educational Development Laboratory, "Harnessing the Power of Beliefs," in *Insights*, Number 11, July 1989.) The work upon which this publication is based was performed pursuant to contract No. 400-83-0007 of the National Institute of Education. It does not, however, necessarily reflect the views of that agency.

APPENDIX B

Organizational Culture Test

(1) List the beliefs that drive your organization.

(2) How are these beliefs communicated?

(3) Are the beliefs reinforced by formal personnel processes, recognition, and rewards?

(4) Do the beliefs affect the day-to-day operations of the organization? If so, how?

(5) Who are the heros in the organization?

(6) What stories are told about the organization by "insiders"

(7) What are the rites (customary expectations of members of this organization, e.g., teachers taking attendance, giving tests, checking homework) of the position holders in this organization?

(8) What are the rituals (ceremonial activities of the organization, e.g., graduation, homecoming games) of the organization? Analyze the rites and rituals to understand what is important in the organization.

Note: Data gathered must be analyzed carefully in order to understand the culture as it currently exists. Beliefs are central and should be analyzed for information such as what beliefs are held in common, who knows the common beliefs, how many members of the organization know the common beliefs, and what the heroes of the organization reveal about the culture of the organization (for example, are shirkers revered, admired?). Similarly, what do the stories, rites and rituals reveal about the organization?

APPENDIX C

Examples of Authentic Assessment

Following are examples of authentic assessment possibilities for various subjects. Note that in several instances the product for assessment is the culmination of a student project. Typically, authentic assessments are graded on a five- to six-point scale with specific descriptors given for each of the levels. Below is a sample of descriptors given in a social studies class:

- A level—Information is drawn from a number of sources, not merely books or articles. Information has been applied in a creative manner and directly addresses the issue or problem that is the focus of the study. A thorough grasp of the problem is demonstrated by presenting various aspects and viewpoints. Analyses and solutions (if a solution is presented) also demonstrate a variety of viewpoints.
- B level—Information is drawn from a number of sources, but mostly confined to books and articles. Information has been applied in a moderately unique manner and generally addresses the issue or problem. Some aspects of the problem are presented, but of these some may be fairly shallow. Analyses and solutions demonstrate several viewpoints, but some are uneven in an understanding of the various positions.
- C level—Information is drawn from several sources and those used are the most common ones. Information has been applied in a routine manner with some inaccuracies. Few aspects of the problem are presented, and those that are presented are fairly shallow. Analyses and solutions demonstrate a single viewpoint.
- D level—Information is drawn from few sources.

Information is brief and may be inappropriately applied to the problem or question. A single aspect of the problem is presented and contains clear biases. Analysis is shallow and biased.

- F level—Report may be late. Information is brief and drawn from one or two sources. May or may not relate to the problem. Analysis may be omitted or brief, shallow, and/or biased.

Using this scale, the teacher can apply reasonably uniform criteria in assigning grades to various student projects, demonstrations, portfolios, proposals, and so forth.

Below are several authentic assessment items. Some are test items and some are projects that students might pursue over a period of time. Both types, however, share the viewpoint that a true assessment asks the student to do something with information, not merely exhibit recall. These items have been excerpted from "A Sampler of Authentic Assessment: What It Is and What It Looks Like," by Ruth Mitchell. This document was prepared for the *Beyond the Bubble Conference* held in Sacramento, California, on October 15-17, 1989.

A Unit-Ending Simulation in High School Economics

You are the president of a large company that is facing a major surplus of products that you are unable to sell. Will a cutback in production work? Your major task is to get your company into a good financial position. If you are successful, you will be given a large bonus. If you are unsuccessful, you will be fired. Prepare a presentation to your Board of Directors.

- Market research shows that for every $1.00 rise in price, 500 less of the product will be demanded. You want to supply 700 units for every dollar rise in price.
  - Develop formulae for demand, supply, equilibrium
  - Graph the company's position
- If you are a monopoly, will this change the way you would solve this problem?
- If you have a surplus
  - What will happen to your workers?
  - What will happen to companies that produce complementary products?

– If you are forced out of the business, what will happen to companies that produce substitute products?
– What could this do to the entire economy?
– How could the government help in this situation?

A Unit Final in a Junior High School Music Appreciation Course

Your group is now a performing jazz group (you may choose your own name). You are going to write a letter to a record company (pick any you like) to ask for a live audition – not a taped one. You will persuade the company that your jazz music is fresh and new and should be heard live by describing it in the technical stylistic terms we have used in class. Compare your music to that of the great players you have heard so that the record company can get a clear idea of your place in the jazz tradition.

An Exercise in Statistical Understanding

In order for students to understand how statistics apparently lie, they were asked to manipulate statistical material themselves by doing this exercise.

In a certain country the defense budget was $30 million for 1989. The total budget for the same year was $500 million. The following year the defense budget was $35 million, and the total budget was $605 million. Inflation between the two budgets was 10 percent.

- You are invited to give a lecture to a pacifist society. You want to explain that the defense budget has been decreasing this year. Explain how to do this.
- You are invited to lecture to a military academy. You want to explain that the defense budget has been increasing this year. Explain how to do this.

A Geography Assessment for a Junior High School Class

You have lived in Mexico City for the past two years. Your cousin Michael is coming to visit you. You are to write a letter to prepare him for his trip. Listed below are the topics you may wish to include in your letter. You are required to include the ones with an asterisk.

(*1) What documents will Michael need to enter the country and how can he obtain them?
(*2) Describe the climate of the area for Michael and make suggestions for the types of clothing he should pack for his trip.

(*3) Tell Michael how to find the current rate of exchange for the U.S. dollar. Acquaint him with the Mexican peso.

(4) Describe for Michael some of the many historic landmarks of Mexico City.

(5) Describe for Michael the landforms and the important bodies of water in the area.

(6) Describe for Michael the new foods he can expect to sample when he visits.

(7) Describe for Michael the different holidays and celebrations observed by the Mexican people.

(*8) Attach to your letter an outline map of North America including Mexico. Note for Michael the location of the country of Mexico and Mexico City. Label the countries and bodies of water that border Mexico.

APPENDIX D

Teaching about Thinking

The schemes for thinking listed below are examples of the kinds of thinking skills that may be used to foster the development of human resources in the classroom.

CoRT I Tools—Breadth

- CAF (Consider All Factors)—encourages students to consider as many factors as possible in trying to further understand reasons for actions or outcomes. Thinking is creative as well as factual.
- FIP (First Important Priorities)—requires students to prioritize among a number of possible reasons for observed or reported outcomes with an accompanying rationale.
- PMI (Plus, Minus, Interesting Points)—permits student to comment on the positive, negative, and interesting points of an event or information.
- C+S (Consequence and Sequel)—allows students to speculate on the outcomes of certain actions or the future of certain courses of action (or hypothetical actions).
- AGO (Aims, Goals, and Objectives)—has students contemplate the objectives of certain actions or observed outcomes.
- APC (Alternatives, Possibilities, Choices)—suggests students generate alternatives to actions taken or decisions made or outcomes observed.
- OPV (Other Points of View)—leads students to consider another point of view rather than their own or that presented by a historical, literary, or scientific actor.

Note that the CoRT skills could be equally applied in literature, social studies, science, or math to engage more deeply with the content. Other CoRT tools include Organization, Interaction, Creativity, Information and Feeling, and Action. Additional information may be obtained from The CoRT Thinking Program, Dormac, Inc., P.O. Box 270459, San Diego, CA 92128-0983.

Tactics for Thinking

- Learning to Learn Skills – attention control, deep processing, memory frameworks, power thinking, goal-setting, and the responsibility frame
- Content Thinking Skills – concept attainment, concept development, pattern recognition, macro-pattern recognition, synthesizing, proceduralizing
- Reasoning Skills – analogical reasoning, extrapolation, evaluation of evidence, examination of value, decision making, nonlinguistic patterns, elaboration, solving everyday problems, solving academic problems, invention

Additional information may be obtained from Marzano, R. and D. Arredondo. 1986. *Tactics for Thinking*. Alexandria, VA: Association for Supervision and Curriculum Development.

Talents Unlimited

This program nurtures student thinking ability in five talent areas:

- Productive Thinking – generating many varied and unusual ideas and adding onto those ideas to improve them
- Communication – conveying needs, feelings, and ideas effectively to others. Related skills include description, comparison, empathy, nonverbal communication, and networking ideas.
- Forecasting – looking into the future to predict things that might happen or looking into the past to consider what might have happened. Forecasting involves predicting both cause and effect relationships.
- Decision Making – having students think of many possible things they could do, asking them to think more carefully about each of these things, letting them choose one, and having them give many varied reasons for their choices
- Effective Planning – deciding what is going to be planned; listing all the resources needed; telling, in order, the steps

taken to complete the plan; describing any problems that might come up during implementation

Further information on the Talents Unlimited program may be obtained from Talents Unlimited, 1107 Arlington St., Mobile, AL 36605.

APPENDIX E

Pampa 2000: Pampa Independent School District Strategic Planning

SIX STEPS TO SUCCEED WITH ACTION PLANS

Can *all* of the children in second grade in Pampa really graduate from high school in the year 2000? Is it possible that our district could have almost every child go on to post-secondary training or school or on to gainful employment in the year 2000? Can we actually improve the self-esteem of *every* child in the next year or two? Can we be a school district that regularly produces high achieving national merit scholars by the year 1993?

I think the answer to each of these questions is YES! It is yes because of many reasons, but foremost because of the quality teachers, administrators, and staff within the Pampa ISD. In addition, we are fortunate to have a community of citizens who are willing to volunteer thousands of hours and commit the resources of our community for an educational program that seeks to insure the success of every child in our community.

SIX STEPS TO SUCCESS

Establishing a *process* to achieve our strategic objectives is critical to the overall success of our strategic plan. Our four objectives are aggressive, but they can be achieved. They can be achieved because of the value that we place on succeeding with every child, on the skills we have for facilitating the success of our teachers, and because of the attention we give to following a useful system for developing effective plans.

1. Determine the outcome (goal).
   a. Clarify, review, and edit the action plans.
      – The action teams did a lot of analysis and gathered a lot of

facts of what needed to be done. The plans need to be carefully reviewed for their content. Do they consist of enough action steps to clearly describe *what* is to be accomplished?

b. Set the outcomes (goal).
  – What is the specific outcome of the action plan? Do outcomes indicate what is to be desired? Specifically, what will have been accomplished – *What will be different?* – when the action plan is completed? Dr. Candoli referred to this as the "product."

c. Determine when and how outcomes (goals) will be measured.
  – This involves setting specific *standards* against which actual progress will be measured. The standards indicate what will be measured and when it will be measured. They are to be written, specific, realistic, and measurable. Sources of information are to be identified.

2. Schedule the action plans.
  a. Break the action step down into a series of events or mileposts.
  b. Place a time estimate on the activity required to move from one event to the next.
  c. Determine which action steps and/or events must be done in *sequence* and which ones can be *parallel with* or *independent* of one another.
  d. Determine the sequence of events which comprises the longest length of time. This is the *critical path* that must be accomplished.

3. Provide for adequate control and accountability.
  a. Decide what kind of decisions are needed, when they are needed, and where in the organization they should be made.
  c. Who will review actions taken to insure that they are of appropriate quality?
  d. Who will see that the action steps/events are actually accomplished?

4. Define resources needed to support the action plans.
  a. What resources are needed in terms of numbers of people, estimated hours, training, materials, equipment, etc.?
  b. Also, who will do what for how long with what resources?

5. Review the plan, action steps, and resource commitments.
  a. How does the plan relate to other events and activities; will modifications be needed?

b. Will follow-up planning be required?

c. Are there some other operational areas which need to be changed as a result of this plan? If so, when?

6. Commit to the plan.

    a. Provide the daily leadership that models belief in the importance of the plan.

    b. Keep the plan in the forefront!

    c. Celebrate successes along the way!!!

Testing the Soundness of Planning

I. Is it consistent with the principles of participatory management?

II. Is it consistent with our strategic parameters?

"We will never allow failure to be final for any student."

"We will always base major program changes on current, accurate and sufficient data to justify the changes."

III. Rules for planning

    a. Grocery Store Rule:

    Is the sequence of activities logical?

    b. Efficiency Rule:

    Are efforts redundant of others? Are similar efforts grouped together?

    c. Is Anyone Home Rule:

    Is the planning sensitive to the availability of key equipment, facilities, and personnel?

    d. Decision-Making Rule:

    Does it meet key event deadlines (the end of tone plan may be the beginning of another)?

    Recognize the impact of one decision on another (until A is finished the next step B, is unclear)

IV. Politically sensitive

Have we "conditioned the turf "?

Are the planning efforts sensitive to the reasons for opposition to change, to the need for further discussion and training, and to giving staff the opportunity to participate?

Are we a "shared responsibility team"?

Are the right groups of teachers, staff, and community citizens involved at the right stages of planning and implementation?

APPENDIX F

Strategies

(1) We will develop and implement a comprehensive at-risk plan for the Pre-K through 12th grades based on the work of the At-Risk Task Force and information gathered by PISD.
(2) We will construct an instructional management system that recognizes and addresses the unique characteristics of all populations of students.
(3) We will identify, develop, and implement strong, continuing staff development programs for teachers of math, English, and special populations.
(4) We will identify, develop, and implement a study and test-taking skills program at appropriate levels.
(5) We will use the diverse human resources in our community to support and strengthen our educational program by working cooperatively with families, educators, and students to
  • provide additional classroom support
  • promote career opportunities
  • assist in strengthening family involvement
  • convince parents of the value of education
(6) We will develop and implement a volunteer program in our schools.
(7) We will develop and implement a program that nurtures the development of positive self-esteem in grades K-12.
(8) We will broaden, strengthen, and intensify the honors curriculum to insure excellence in our honors program

Pampa ISD

Examples of Action Plans

  • transition programs for elementary to middle school, middle school to high school

- maintaining parental involvement
- teacher exchanges
- staff development
  - policy revision
  - teacher grant program
  - departmental exchanges
- community speaker bureau
- teacher self-esteem program
- instructional management program
- early identification of honors students
- extensive revision of honors curriculum
- classroom volunteers
- districtwide study and test-taking skills program
- numerous at-risk programs
  - peer tutors
  - student support groups

Action Plan: Instructional Management

Over-Arching Goal

Every student will perform in mathematics at grade level or above, every year.

Two Phases

I. Readiness and awareness of campus level teachers to IMS
II. Implementation of IMS

Outcome

Phase I–to involve teachers in an awareness and commitments to implementation of instructional management system
Phase II–determine outcome

1. Learn to value mathematics (intrinsic)
   a. Measure by three-question survey
   b. Measure by interview

2. Learn to reason mathematically (problem solving)
   a. Measure by individual student computer report
   b. Measure by improved test outcomes

3. Learn to communicate mathematically
   a. Be able to relate to real world situations

   b. Classroom extension activities
   c. Parent, teacher, student observations
4. Become confident of their own math abilities
   a. Incrased student involvement in math (activities UIL)
   b. Teachers observation
5. Become math problem solvers
   a. Increased mastery of stated problems
   b. Monitored individualized date
6. Every student accountable and responsible for learning
   a. 80% mastery of each unit
   b. Students move at individual pace

Activity	Person Resp.	Date	Resources	Evaluation
Plan with campus rep. of Inst. Manag. Task Force to review action plan for presentation to faculty	Principal/Campus Rep.	Aug. 22	Action team reports "six steps to success"	Feedback
Present action plan to faculty	Principal/ Campus Rep.	Aug. 28	Action team reports "six steps to success"	
Review evaluation for success	Principal Team Leader		Teacher eval.	
Faculty mtg. to review & discuss results of teacher in-service	Principal Team Leader	Sept.	Feedback report	
Campus rep. selected for leader council	Principal Team Leader	Sept.		
Faculty rep. meets with leader council	Asst. Supt.	Oct.	Task Force report; other as needed	
Faculty rep. reports to faculty	Inst. Leadership Rep.	Oct.	Report from district meeting	
Faculty rep. takes info. to dist.mtg.	Inst. Leadership Rep.	Oct./ Monthly meeting		
Parent reps. on task force meet with principal and team leader	Principal & parent rep	Nov.		

(continued)

Activity	Person Resp.	Date	Resources	Evatuation
Parent rep. & team leader report to faculty to prepare for parent mtg.	Parent rep. & Team Leader	Nov. & Dec.		
Parent mtg. to acquaint with IMS	Principal, Parent rep. & Team Leader	Feb.	Task Force Report	
Discussion of IMS at faculty meeting	Principal, Parent rep. & Team Leader	Feb. & May	As needed	
Select rep. for dist. wide development tests	Campus rep.	June & Aug.		
Campus rep. work on developing test	Campus rep.	June & Aug.		
Campus rep. reports to faculty	Principal/ Campus rep.	Sept.		

APPENDIX G

A Sample of Belief Statements

The following beliefs were tested against the criteria below before they were accepted.

Criteria

- *Relevance*—Is this a fundamental, core belief?
- *Importance*—Would its acceptance make a difference?
- *Common meaning*—Can it be readily understood by the average person?
- *Context*—Does the statement fit within the context of the whole set?
- *Universality*—Can the belief be applied at all levels (school, district, state) to all involved (students, teachers, administrators, parents, school board members, etc.) and in all areas (curriculum, instruction, staff development, budgeting, etc.)?

Declaration of Intent

Every individual has a vested interest in the success of schooling. To insure that success, we must build a system based on vision and moral purpose. Our intent must be to restructure the educational system into a learning community that supports, affirms, and reflects in its every operation the following fundamental beliefs.[3]

---

[3] Adapted from working papers of the Texas/SEDL Organizing for Excellence Partners, 1989. Southwest Educational Development Laboratory, 211 E. 7th St., Austin, TX 78701.

Beliefs

(1) All people have equal value and worth.

(2) Every person can learn and realize success.

(3) Together, the family, the school, and the community control the conditions for success.

(4) Schools must develop knowledge, skills, thinking processes, and attitudes for successful living today and for tomorrow's world.

(5) In a democratic society, schools must ensure the opportunities necessary for all individuals to reach their potential.

(6) Schools must enable individuals to assume responsibility for their own behavior and performance.

(7) Schools that honor courtesy, mutual respect, obligation, and shared commitment provide the best conditions for success.

(8) Collaboration and cooperation are essential for arriving at the best decisions and for implementing successful solutions.

(9) Individuals and schools must be empowered with sufficient authority to carry out responsibilities for which they are held accountable.

(10) Successful schools require a climate that encourages creativity and innovation.

APPENDIX H

Using Statements of Basic Belief to Audit the System

Belief Statement (Compose a belief statement here.)

Area of Audit (Write the area to be audited here – see list below.)

Statements of basic belief should apply to every level of the system, to all areas (see below), and to all involved in the schooling effort. Every policy, practice, rule, or procedure should support one or more of the statements. If one does not, the list of statements of belief should be examined for completeness and the policy, practice, rule, or procedure should be examined for validity. Likewise, a policy, practice, rule, or procedure should not contradict any statement of belief. If it does, both the statement and the policy, practice, rule, or procedure should be examined for validity. As a result of such an audit, changes should be made in both the statements of belief and the policies, practices, rules, and procedures to ensure they are in agreement.

Areas to be audited might include the following[4]:

- school board policies
- rules and regulations at all levels
- budgeting procedures
- curriculum
- instructional practices
- disciplinary procedures
- personnel assessment
- student assessment
- scheduling
- staff assignment
- resource allocation
- decision-making process

[4] Adapted from Southwest Educational Development Laboratory. 1989. "Using Statements of Basic Belief to Audit the System."

APPENDIX I

Sample Discrepancy Analysis

A discrepancy analysis displays the difference between a current state and a desired state. By utilizing the discrepancy model, it is possible to identify the areas of greatest concern. Focusing on these areas to begin with assures the leader of a broad base of support. Respondents may include teachers, administrators, board members, parents, students, and businesspersons.

Directions – Read the statements below. Decide on a scale of 1 (low) to 5 (high) the degree to which the statement is a *desired* condition in your district and so indicate in the blank on the *left*. Then, using the same scale, decide the degree to which it is actually *in place* in your district and so indicate in the blank to the *right*. The results of this survey will be used to identify the focus for improvement in this school district.

DESIRED   IN PLACE

1. _____ Students feel good about themselves and experience success in this district. _____

2. _____ Teachers are trusted to make important decisions in this district. _____

3. _____ Parents are considered to be important members of the learning team. _____

4. _____ The board considers teachers true professionals and treats them accordingly. _____

5. _____ Curriculum is geared to the needs of the 21st century. _____

6. _____ Information is widely available in this district. _____

7. _____ All decisions that can be made at the school level are permitted to be made there. _____

8. _____ Authentic assessments as well as standardized tests are used to evaluate the effectiveness of the school program. _____

9. _____ There is a shared group of beliefs that drive the _____ decisions in this destrict.
10. _____ Decisions are made by consensus (rather than by _____ voting or by the leader alone).

Note: The above statements are for illustrative purposes only. District leaders will need to fashion their own instruments based on the prevailing conditions in their district.

APPENDIX J

Open-ended Statements—Needs/Beliefs

Directions: Below is a series of incomplete statements. Please complete the statements with an ending that is most true for you. This survey will be used to make improvements in the district. Respondents may include teachers, administrators, parents, board members, students, and businesspersons.

1. I understand the main mission of this district is to_____

2. The best way to get ahead in this district is to_____

3. The most admired person in this district is_____

4. The way decisions in this district are made is by_____

5. Teachers in this district are considered to be_____

6. At risk students in this district have_____

7. The curriculum in this district prepares students for_____

8. Parents feel that they have_____

9. The thing that most needs to be changed in this district is_____

10. When change is introduced in this district it is generally_____

Note: This list of questions may be extended to include issues on which responses are needed. Once the answers are received they may be categorized, and a summary developed. The responses may well serve as a catalyst for a clearer statement of beliefs and/or needs.

APPENDIX K

School Restructuring Plan—Phase-in

For a variety of reasons, a district might need to phase in restructuring rather than introducing it all at once. For example, a principal might be close to retirement, a school might be doing well under current organization, or other initiatives may be underway. In the event that a phase-in approach is decided on, the following plan may help anticipate potential problems or avoid unnecessary delays. To begin with, schools should be selected for the first restructuring group. A selected group is preferred because principals and their teachers might have a variety of reasons for volunteering that might not necessarily signal their readiness to begin restructuring. For example, they might volunteer in order to be perceived as on the cutting edge; they might think extra perks will flow to their schools; or they might think they will get the better students. Criteria that might be used in selecting the first schools include

- having a history of successful innovation
- having a history of teacher/parent involvement
- having inquired about restructuring and expressed an interest in it
- having shown initiative in thoughtful responses to district or state mandates
- having emphasized faculty growth on campus (as opposed to attending external workshops)
- having demonstrated concern for/interest in/commitment to children
- having principals who are above average in intelligence and who are highly articulate

The district should have already built a community-wide agreement on the need for change and a base of support. Due to this preparation, school personnel and the public should be anticipating

211

changes in the operation of the schools and should have some understanding of the expected changes. As the first schools are chosen for restructuring, the remaining schools should be told that they will all be expected to move in this direction in order to prepare them and remove the possible sense that this is an experiment that may or may not continue. With this understanding, the schools that are chosen can commit to making the project work; those that are not chosen will likely observe the situation much more closely knowing that they must eventually move in this direction.

During Year One of the implementation, training should be held for the central office staff, building principals, and lead teachers in the skills discussed in Chapter 3 and the understandings on curriculum, instruction, and human cognition discussed in Chapter 4. Training should follow the Joyce-Showers model described in Chapter 8. Not only should training prepare the building principals in the content, but it should prepare them to be trainers in their own buildings. Toward the end of Year One, an orientation session should be held for teachers. Prior to this time, principals may have been holding discussions with their teachers, but this will put the official stamp of the district on the project.

Year Two should be a year of planning for the implementation to take place in Year Three. It should begin with further training for teachers either in the summer or in August in the skills of restructuring as developed in Chapter 3. This is necessary so that the teachers will have the requisite skills to carry out their roles in restructuring. At this time also some information about instruction, human cognition, and curriculum as described in Chapter 4 could be presented. Having established the needs already and knowing the broad goals at the district level, the school faculty can proceed to develop a statement of beliefs such as "We agree" items. It is necessary for the faculty to have a shared, written statement of their fundamental commitments, for it is these that will guide their policy, curriculum, and instructional decisions to follow.

With this philosophy as a guide, a building committee of parents, teachers, and the principal can proceed to review the school curriculum, policies, and instruction. All decisions should be made by consensus. As planning progresses, parents and the central office should be kept informed. Meetings will need to continue in the central office to renew the principals in the contemporary research regarding human cognition, curriculum, and instruction.

Year Two is likely to be marked by increasing enthusiasm as the teachers learn to work together and to exercise their professional skills. Trial units might be developed and taught by volunteer teachers, with critiques provided by other teachers. By the end of Year Two, the school committee should be ready to present its plan to parents, the central office, and the board. Sometime during Year Two, PAL teams should be formed. PAL teams would consist of two or three principals teamed together in order to observe one another in the conduct of the school committee meetings. The team members would then be able to provide formative comments on the skill of the principal being observed and provide suggestions for improvement. Care would have to be exercised to insure that all parties knew the purpose was not to evaluate, but merely to assist the principals in skill development. A final activity in Year Two would be to introduce a new group of principals into the Year One activities.

Year Three would be the year of implementation and refinement. It could also be the year that discouragement surfaces. Implementing plans that combine understandings from human cognition, instruction, and curriculum could prove difficult and time-consuming. Parents and students may well complain when familiar practices are altered. Necessary teacher meetings needed to iron out misunderstandings or coordinate plans may cause a drain on teacher time, the central office may express reservations, and so forth.

A great deal of emotional and physical energy may be saved if the philosophy and the plans that grew out of that philosophy are reviewed at the beginning of the year to ensure that the program is on track. As the year progresses, care will need to be exercised to give wide publicity to the successes of the program, to establish rituals that will sustain the changes, and to plan for rites of celebration as goals are reached. The principal will need to act as cheerleader and continually express his confidence in the program and the teachers. These behaviors will assist in the culture change that will be necessary in order to sustain the program changes.

By the end of Year Three, the initial schools should be ready for site visits by representatives from the schools that started in the process the second year. At this point, more schools may be started in the process and the original schools can continue to refine their programs to bring them into line with their philosophies. Full restructuring will take from three to five years for each school or group of schools from the initial development efforts.

APPENDIX L

The Team Effectiveness Critique

Instructions: Circle the number below that represents your evaluation of the effectiveness of the indicated group functioning characteristic.

1. Goals

GOALS VAGUE, NOT ACCEPTED   GOALS CLEAR, ACCEPTED

| 1 | 2 | 3 | 4 | 5 | 6 | 7 |

2. Utilization of member potential

POORLY UTILIZED   FULLY UTILIZED

| 1 | 2 | 3 | 4 | 5 | 6 | 7 |

3. Trust

LOW TRUST/HIGH COVERT ACTIVITIES   HIGH TRUST/LOW COVERT

| 1 | 2 | 3 | 4 | 5 | 6 | 7 |

4. Conflict

CONFLICT IGNORED/COVERED UP   CONFLICT SURFACED/RESOLVED

| 1 | 2 | 3 | 4 | 5 | 6 | 7 |

5. Balance

DOMINANCE BY A FEW   BALANCED PARTICIPATION

| 1 | 2 | 3 | 4 | 5 | 6 | 7 |

6. Process

DISORGANIZED   ORGANIZED

| 1 | 2 | 3 | 4 | 5 | 6 | 7 |

7. Interpersonal Communications

CLOSED/GUARDED   OPEN/SPONTANEOUS

| 1 | 2 | 3 | 4 | 5 | 6 | 7 |

8. Bounded Decisions

DISTRICT PHILOSOPHY IGNORED   DIST. PHIL. CONSIDERED

| 1 | 2 | 3 | 4 | 5 | 6 | 7 |

9. Policy/Rule Constraint

POLICIES RESTRICT PROPOSALS   ALL PROPOSALS CONSIDERED

| 1 | 2 | 3 | 4 | 5 | 6 | 7 |

APPENDIX M

End-of-Year Assessment

(1) What has been the greatest accomplishment of ILC?

- "One of the greatest accomplishments of ILC was the clarification of the 'Enhanced Learning Time' at the elementary level. I also feel that 'PLATO' was a great accomplishment."
- "Uniting elementary and secondary educators in the direction of viewing our 'district' goals/needs rather than isolated campus goals or needs." (Note: While individual campuses were encouraged to devise local responses to the district core mission, they were not free to devise their own independent missions.)
- "Being able to interact with administrators and teachers from all campuses."
- "Developing a districtwide closeness—being able to discuss openly."

(2) How effective do you feel the decisions and recommendations of the ILC have been in relation to your campus needs?

- "The campus representatives have expressed the concerns of the campus staff. Communication between ILC and staff has improved."
- "I think we have good two-way communication from the campus leadership teams to ILC and vice-versa. Several recommendations have given us many good ideas. ILC's decisions have reflected teachers' feelings on matters."
- "I feel our campus was jealous of the ILC. All of our leadership felt threatened by the items that were discussed. Perhaps hostile would be a better word than threatened. Ideas brought from the ILC were terrific!"

(3) What do you feel you personally contributed to the ILC?

- "I feel I contributed the ideas and views of teachers that teach in the electives. I also feel I have a good understanding of what our business community is looking for in high school graduates and that benefits the ILC."
- "Bringing input from my campus to the ILC and then communicating decisions to the leaderhip team."
- "I think that I've gained many ideas, but also have shared much of the good at-risk planning that we've done at Baker for two years. Our small groups are not afraid to disagree. There are differences of opinion shared openly."

(4) What have you learned from your participation in the ILC?

- "I have enjoyed the opportunity to exchange ideas and listen to teachers in grades K-8. The ILC has been a wonderful opportunity and educational experience. Through ILC I have a better understanding of Pampa district."
- "I gained a vast amount of knowledge about the elementary level of Pampa. It gave me better overall picture of the whole system."
- "I learned that even though the experiences, priorities, and philosophies of the members involved were sometimes evidently varied, the ILC could come to a consensus that would benefit the majority of students and teachers. The ILC bridged a gap that sometimes exists between elementary and secondary teachers."

(5) What recommendations or suggestions do you have to improve the ILC?

- "At this time I do not have any recommendations or suggestions for ILC. I like the way we have operated this past year."
- "I have no recommendations for improvement. I would be happy if we continued in the same manner as we conducted business this year."
- "I guess I never understood why all elementary principals weren't included in the ILC, especially since elementary campuses seemed to be most affected by ILC activities this year."

APPENDIX N

Discrepancy Analysis and Action Planning

The following can be used as headings to develop a discrepancy analysis and action plan:

WHAT IS THE CURRENT SITUATION?

WHAT WOULD BE THE IDEAL SITUATION?

WHAT ARE THE BARRIERS TO ACHIEVING THE IDEAL?

WHAT MUST BE DONE TO OVERCOME THE BARRIERS?

WHAT IS THE BENEFIT OF MOVING TOWARD THE IDEAL?

INDEX